Wash Your Hair

With Whipped Cream

AND HUNDREDS MORE OFFBEAT USES FOR EVEN MORE BRAND-NAME PRODUCTS

Joey Green

HYPERION

New York

Design by Joey Green

Library of Congress Cataloging-in-Publication Data

Green, Joey.
    Wash your hair with whipped cream : and hundreds more offbeat uses for even more brand-name products / Joey Green.
      p. cm.
    Includes bibliographical references and index.
    ISBN 0-7868-8276-X
    1. Home economics. 2. Brand name products—United States. 3. Medicine, Popular.   I. Title
TX158.G686 1997   97-12161
640'.41—dc21   CIP

First Edition
10 9 8 7 6 5 4 3 2 1

For
Minerva and Hank,
Mitzi,
Sylvia and Al,
and Harold and Judy

Ingredients

Yet Another Word From Our Sponsor

I was truly amazed to find myself on the NBC *Today* show and *CNN Headline News* polishing furniture with SPAM. Next thing I knew my picture was in the *New York Times* pouring a can of Coca-Cola into a toilet bowl. And then I was on television again, this time teaching Tammy Faye Baker how to shave with Jif peanut butter. The American public's fascination with the hundreds of quirky uses for brand-name products was bigger than I ever thought possible. I had opened Pandora's box.

In a strange way, I had become a public servant, destined to open the clandestine files on America's favorite brand-name products and share their secrets with the world. After all, the public has a right to know the offbeat uses for products like ChapStick, Dixie Cups, Jell-O, Reddi-wip, and Saran Wrap—although I'm not quite sure you'll find that in the Bill of Rights.

Once again I've discovered some remarkable truths. Tang cleans toilet bowls. Miracle Whip conditions hair. Crisco All-Vegetable Shortening prevents diaper rash. Alberto VO5 Hair Spray removes ink from clothes. Wilson Tennis Balls can be used to baby-proof your home. But I wanted to know much more. How did Wonder Bread get its name? Who is Aunt Jemima? And is she related to Uncle Ben?

Here then are the exciting findings of my third quest into the depths of American myth, legend, and folklore. This time, I had the foresight to include Alka-Seltzer.

Conditioning Hairdressing

■**Prevent silver from tarnishing.** Apply a thin coat of Alberto VO5 Conditioning Hairdressing with a soft cloth to clean, polished, dry silver candlesticks, picture frames, silver sets, and other decorative items. Wipe off excess, leaving behind a very thin, virtually invisible, protective coating. VO5's organic protectants actually prevent tarnishing.

■**Remove a ring stuck on a finger.** Rub on a little Alberto VO5 Conditioning Hairdressing, then hold your hand up toward the ceiling to drain the blood from the area and slide off the ring.

■**Make cleaning up after painting or doing a messy auto grease job easy.** Lightly coating your hands with Alberto VO5 Conditioning Hairdressing before painting or fixing the car allows you to clean them off afterward without harsh solvents.

■ **Soften your feet.** Before going to bed, coat your feet with Alberto VO5 Conditioning Hairdressing and put on a pair of socks.

■ **Soften dry cuticles and moisturize dry elbows and heels.** Rub on a dab of Alberto VO5 Conditioning Hairdressing.

■ **Prevent spray paint from sticking in your hair.** Before spray painting, slick a dab of Alberto VO5 Conditioning Hairdressing the size of a quarter over your hair so you can wash away the paint more easily.

■ **Prevent static electricity in your hair.** Comb a dab of Alberto VO5 Conditioning Hairdressing through your hair.

■ **Protect your scalp during a permanent.** Rub some Alberto VO5 Conditioning Hairdressing into the scalp before giving yourself a perm.

■ **Minimize drying out your hair in a chlorinated pool.** Rub a long dab of Alberto VO5 Conditioning Hairdressing through your hair before taking a swim.

■ **Prevent hair coloring from dyeing your skin.** Dab a little Alberto VO5 Conditioning Hairdressing on your forehead and around the hairline and ears to help keep the color from staining your skin.

■ **Remove makeup.** A dab of Alberto VO5 Conditioning Hairdressing on a tissue or cotton ball gently removes makeup.

■ **Glitter your face for a holiday party.** Rub a little Alberto VO5 Conditioning Hairdressing onto your cheeks, then dust lightly with glitter.

■ **Moisturize your face.** Rub a little Alberto VO5 Conditioning Hairdressing in the lines around your eyes to help prevent dry lines.

■ **Remove an adhesive bandage painlessly.** Rub a little Alberto VO5 Conditioning Hairdressing into the bandage wings, wait a few minutes, then peel off.

■ **Soothe chapped lips and skin.** Rub in a small amount of Alberto VO5 Conditioning Hairdressing.

■ **Soothe your legs after shaving.** Rub some Alberto VO5 Conditioning Hairdressing into your skin after a bath or shower to make your legs feel velvety smooth.

■ **Make zippers glide easily.** Rub a little Alberto VO5 Conditioning Hairdressing into the teeth of the zipper.

■ **Condition leather.** If you're all out of mink oil, substitute Alberto VO5 Conditioning Hairdressing.

■ **Protect leather shoes and boots from winter salt and ice.** Rub in Alberto VO5 Conditioning Hairdressing.

■ **Shine vinyl and patent leather shoes.** Rub in a little Alberto VO5 Conditioning Hairdressing, then buff.

■ **Protect your dog's or cat's paw pads.** Rub in a little

Alberto VO5 Conditioning Hairdressing before sending your pet outdoors.

■ **Prevent shoes from squeaking.** Give squeaky shoes a coat of Alberto VO5 Conditioning Hairdressing.

■ **Detangle and shine a dog's coat.** Comb in a small amount of Alberto VO5 Conditioning Hairdressing.

■ **Prevent cat hair balls and static electricity on your cat's coat.** Rub in a little Alberto VO5 Conditioning Hairdressing. (Don't worry if your cat licks its fur; Alberto VO5 Conditioning Hairdressing is natural and nontoxic.)

■ **Shine a horse's hooves.** Rub in a little Alberto VO5 Conditioning Hairdressing.

■ **Prevent a leather saddle from drying out.** Rub in a little Alberto VO5 Conditioning Hairdressing.

■ **Detangle a horse's mane and tail.** Brush in a little Alberto VO5 Conditioning Hairdressing.

■ **Stop windows from sticking in their tracks.** Lubricate the tracks with a little Alberto VO5 Conditioning Hairdressing.

■ **Lubricate pipe joints.** A thin layer of Alberto VO5 Conditioning Hairdressing on pipe connections will make them fit together more easily.

■ **Prevent nuts and bolts from rusting together.**

Lubricate the nuts and bolts with a dab of Alberto VO5 Conditioning Hairdressing before screwing them together.

■ **Prevent tools from rusting.** Give your tools a light coat of Alberto VO5 Conditioning Hairdressing.

■ **Stop a faucet from screeching.** Remove the handle and stem, coat both sets of metal threads with Alberto VO5 Conditioning Hairdressing, and replace.

■ **Stop refrigerator racks from sticking.** Coat the edges of the racks with a thin layer of Alberto VO5 Conditioning Hairdressing so the racks glide easily.

■ **Prevent squeaky door hinges.** Apply a little bit of Alberto VO5 Conditioning Hairdressing.

■ **Lubricate furniture drawers.** Rub a little Alberto VO5 Conditioning Hairdressing on the casters of drawers so they slide open and shut easily.

■ **Keep shower curtains gliding easily.** Apply a thin coat of Alberto VO5 Conditioning Hairdressing to the curtain rod.

■ **Prevent sliding doors on a medicine cabinet from sticking.** Rub a little Alberto VO5 Conditioning Hairdressing onto the glides.

■ **Clean wooden knickknacks and other wood objects.** Lightly coat the wood with Alberto VO5 Conditioning Hairdressing, then buff.

■ **Avoid splattering paint on windows, hinges, door-knobs, and lock latches.** Coat them with Alberto VO5 Conditioning Hairdressing to prevent paint from adhering to the surfaces. After painting, wipe clean with a cloth.

■ **Hide scratches on wood furniture.** Put a dab of Alberto VO5 Conditioning Hairdressing on a clean, soft cloth, then buff the spot.

■ **Prevent wood paneling from drying out.** Just rub on Alberto VO5 Conditioning Hairdressing with a clean, soft cloth, then buff well, giving the paneling a soft glow.

■ **Remove wax drippings from candlestick holders.** Coat the candlestick holders with Alberto VO5 Conditioning Hairdressing before inserting the candles.

■ **Make a stainless steel sink sparkle.** Shine the sink with a dab of Alberto VO5 Conditioning Hairdressing on a soft cloth.

■ **Shine chrome faucets, handles, and car bumpers.** Put a little Alberto VO5 Conditioning Hairdressing on a soft, dry cloth and buff lightly.

■ **Clean plant leaves.** Apply a small dab of Alberto VO5 Conditioning Hairdressing to the leaves with a soft cloth.

■ **Break in a baseball glove.** Rub the center of the glove with Alberto VO5 Conditioning Hairdressing, place a baseball in the glove, fold the mitt around it, and secure with rubber bands. Tuck the glove under a mattress overnight.

■ **Lubricate roller skates, skateboard wheels, and bicycle chains.** Use a dab of Alberto VO5 Conditioning Hairdressing.

■ **Prevent a sailboat's spinnaker pole fittings from jamming or sticking.** Lubricate with Alberto VO5 Conditioning Hairdressing.

■ **Make golf clubs shine.** Clean the shafts with a dab of Alberto VO5 Conditioning Hairdressing on a clean cloth.

Invented
1956

The Name
Alberto VO5 is named after Alberto, the chemist who invented Alberto VO5 Conditioning Hairdressing. "VO5" stands for the five *v*ital *o*rganic emollients in the hairdressing. Oddly, no one at Alberto-Culver can recall Alberto's first name.

A Short History
In the 1950s, a chemist named Alberto developed Alberto VO5 Conditioning Hairdressing to rejuvenate the coiffures of Hollywood's movie stars from the damage of harsh studio lights. The five vital organic emollients in Alberto VO5 Conditioning Hairdressing restore resiliency and flexibility to dull, dry hair, smooth frizzies and split ends, help control static flyaway, and protect hair from further damage.

Alberto's partner, Blaine Culver, marketed the company until 1955, when thirty-six-year-old Leonard Lavin and his wife, Bernice, bought the Los Angeles–based beauty supply firm for $400,000 and relocated it to Chicago. That same year, the company ran the first television commercial for VO5, and within three years Alberto VO5 Conditioning Hairdressing was the best–selling hair conditioner in the United States.

Ingredients

Mineral oil, petrolatum, lanolin, PEG-8 dilaurate, paraffin, isopropyl myristate, fragrance, BHA

Strange Fact

■ In 1972, Alberto-Culver changed advertising by combining two thirty-second television commercials into the industry's first sixty-second spot.

Distribution

■ Alberto VO5 is the number-one hair conditioner in the United States.

■ Alberto VO5 Conditioning Hairdressing is available in Normal Formula, Gray Formula, Extra Body, and Unscented Formula.

■ Alberto-Culver markets Alberto VO5 shampoos and hair treatments, SugarTwin sweetener, Mrs. Dash seasonings, and Kleen Guard furniture polish.

■ Alberto-Culver owns the world's largest chain of beauty supply stores, Sally Beauty Supply. Sally Beauty operates more than 1,400 outlets offering salon products and appliances to professional and retail customers.

■ Alberto-Culver sells its personal use products in more than 100 countries.

For More Information

Alberto-Culver USA, Inc., 2525 Armitage Avenue, Melrose Park, IL 60160. Or telephone 1-708-450-3000.

Hair Spray

■**Immobilize flying insects.** Spray Alberto VO5 Hair Spray on a flying insect to stiffen its wings, bringing the pest spiraling to the ground.

■**Protect artwork.** When sprayed on a chalk drawing, Alberto VO5 Hair Spray acts as a fixative, preventing artwork from fading.

■**Remove ink stains from clothes, vinyl, or skin.** Spray Alberto VO5 Hair Spray on the stain, blot until the stain comes up, and wash.

■**Kill plant lice on African violets.** Spray Alberto VO5 Hair Spray into a plastic bag (not directly onto the plant), place the bag over the plant, secure shut with a twist tie, and let sit overnight.

■**Thread a needle.** Stiffen the end of the thread with Alberto VO5 Hair Spray so it can be easily poked through the eye of a needle.

■**Laminate recipe cards.** Spray with Alberto VO5 Hair Spray to give the cards a protective gloss.

■**Stiffen ruffled curtains.** Hold the fabric taut and spray with Alberto VO5 Hair Spray.

■ **Preserve floral arrangements.** Spray Alberto VO5 Hair Spray on baby's breath, broom grass, and cattails to help preserve them.

■ **Make wrapping paper.** Spray Alberto VO5 Hair Spray on the comics section from the Sunday paper to seal in the ink and give the paper a shiny gloss.

■ **Remove dry glue from bottles.** Spray Alberto VO5 Hair Spray on the dry glue, wipe off, and wash the bottle in soapy water. The propanes, butanes, and acetones in Alberto VO5 Hair Spray dissolve glue.

■ **Remove pet hair from furniture.** Spray a tissue with Alberto VO5 Hair Spray and, while the tissue is sticky, pick up those hairs.

■ **Protect decorative copper or brass from tarnish.** After polishing decorative copper or brass, spray with Alberto VO5 Hair Spray to add a protective coating.

Invented
1961

The Name

Alberto VO5 is named after Alberto, the chemist who invented Alberto VO5 Conditioning Hairdressing. "VO5" stands for the five *v*ital *o*rganic emollients in the hairdressing. Oddly, no one at Alberto-Culver can recall Alberto's first name.

A Short History

A chemist named Alberto developed Alberto VO5 Conditioning Hairdressing to rejuvenate the coiffures of Hollywood's movie stars from the damage of harsh studio lights. Alberto's business partner, Blaine Culver, marketed the company. In 1955, Leonard Lavin and his wife, Bernice, bought the Los Angeles–based beauty supply firm that manufactured VO5 from Blaine Culver for $400,000 and relocated it to Chicago. That same year the company ran the first television commercial for VO5, and within three years Alberto VO5 Conditioning Hairdressing was the best–selling hair conditioner in the United States.

In 1960, Alberto-Culver built a new plant and headquarters in Melrose, Illinois, and the company went public the following year. Alberto-Culver introduced Alberto VO5 Hair Spray in 1961, Alberto VO5 shampoo in 1962, New Dawn hair color in 1963, and FDS in 1966. Leonard Lavin's son-in-law and daughter, Howard and Carol Bernick, assumed management of Alberto-Culver in 1992. Two years later, Howard Bernick was named CEO, and Carol Bernick became president of the Alberto-Culver USA unit.

Ingredients

SD alcohol 40, dimethyl ether, water, butane, octyl-acrylamide/acrylates/butylaminoethyl methacrylate copolymer, vinyl acetale/crotonates/vinyl neodecanoate copolymer/amino-methyl propanol, dimethyl stearamine, fragrance, MEA-borate, MIPA-borate

Strange Facts

■ Alberto VO5 Hair Spray was the world's first crystal-clear hair spray.

■ In 1972, Alberto-Culver changed advertising by putting two thirty-second television commercials together and creating the industry's first sixty-second spot.

Distribution

■ Alberto-Culver markets Alberto VO5 shampoos and hair treatments, SugarTwin sweetener, Mrs. Dash seasonings, and Kleen Guard furniture polish.

■ Alberto-Culver owns the world's largest chain of beauty supply stores, Sally Beauty Supply. Sally Beauty operates more than 1,400 outlets offering salon products and appliances to professional and retail customers.

■ Alberto-Culver sells its personal use products in more than 100 countries.

For More Information

Alberto-Culver USA, Inc., 2525 Armitage Avenue, Melrose Park, IL 60160. Or telephone 1-708-450-3000.

■ Clean a toilet. Drop in two Alka-Seltzer tablets, wait twenty minutes, brush, and flush. The citric acid and effervescent action clean vitreous china.

■ Clean a vase. To remove a stain from the bottom of a glass vase or cruet, fill with water and drop in two Alka-Seltzer tablets.

■ Polish jewelry. Drop two Alka-Seltzer tablets into a glass of water and immerse the jewelry for two minutes.

■ Clean a thermos bottle. Fill the bottle with water, drop in four Alka-Seltzer tablets, and let soak for an hour (or longer, if necessary).

■ Remove burned-on grease from a pot or pan. Fill the pot or pan with water, drop in six Alka-Seltzer tablets, let soak for one hour, then scrub as usual.

■ Unclog a drain. Clear the sink drain by dropping three Alka-Seltzer tablets down the drain followed by a cup of Heinz White Vinegar. Wait a few minutes, then run the hot water.

■ Get short-term relief from nicotine withdrawal symptoms. As long as you're not on a low-sodium diet or have peptic ulcers, drink two Alka-Seltzer tablets dissolved in a glass of water at every meal.

■ **Soothe insect bites.** Dissolve two Alka-Seltzer tablets in a glass of water, dip a cloth into the solution, and place the cloth on the bite for twenty minutes.

Invented
1930

The Name
Alka-Seltzer is a coined word that suggests *alka*linity and the carbonation of *seltzer*.

A Short History
In 1928, Hub Beardsley, president of Dr. Miles Laboratories, discovered that the editor of the local newspaper in Elkhart, Indiana, prevented his staff from getting influenza during a severe flu epidemic by giving them a novel combination of aspirin and baking soda. Beardsley immediately set his chief chemist, Maurice Treneer, to work devising a tablet containing the two ingredients.

In 1978, Bayer acquired Miles Laboratories. Bayer, founded by Friedrich Bayer in 1863 to develop synthetic dyes, became a pioneer in the modern German chemical industry—developing the first synthetic pesticide in 1892, aspirin in 1899, synthetic rubber in 1915, a treatment for African sleeping sickness in 1921, and the first sulfa drug in 1935—and pioneered the development of polyurethanes. In 1992, Bayer merged its U.S. holdings—Miles Laboratories, Mobay, Agfa, and management holding company Bayer USA—under the name Miles, Inc. In 1994, Bayer acquired the North American over-the-counter drug company Sterling Winthrop, paving the way for the company to change Miles, Inc.'s name to Bayer Corporation.

Ingredients

Each Alka-Seltzer tablet contains 325 milligrams of aspirin, 1,916 milligrams of heat-treated sodium bicarbonate, and 1,000 milligrams of citric acid. Alka-Seltzer in four ounces of water contains principally the antacid sodium citrate and the analgesic sodium acetylsalicylate.

Strange Facts

■ An Alka-Seltzer tablet fizzing in a glass of water prompted a hung-over W. C. Fields to joke, "Can't anyone do something about that racket?"

■ Early promotions for Alka-Seltzer featured Speedy Alka-Seltzer, a baby-faced puppet with red hair and a tablet-shaped hat, created in 1951. Stop-motion animation brought Speedy to life in 212 television commercials between 1954 and 1964, requiring nineteen plaster heads with various lip positions, two sets of legs and arms, and as many as 1,440 adjustments for a single sixty-second commercial. Voice-over talent Dick Beals provided Speedy's voice. Speedy Alka-Seltzer co-starred with Buster Keaton, Martha Tilton, Sammy Davis Jr., and the Flintstones. Speedy Alka-Seltzer celebrated America's Bicentennial, participated in the 1980 Winter Olympics, attended thousands of holiday dinners, and has helped Santa Claus.

■ The original six-inch-high Speedy Alka-Seltzer working model became so famous that it was insured for $100,000 and kept in the vault of a Beverly Hills bank. In 1955, a plastic Speedy doll was issued in a limited edition.

■ The buffered aspirin in Alka-Seltzer peaks within thirty minutes, whereas regular aspirin tablets peak in about two hours.

■ In the 1970s, Alka-Seltzer became widely known for its innovative television commercials, launching the catchphrases "Mama mia, that's a spicy meatball," "Try it, you'll like it," and "I can't believe I ate the whole thing."

■ The "Plop, Plop, Fizz, Fizz, Oh, What a Relief It Is!" vintage theme song for Alka-Seltzer, written by Tom Dawes in 1977, remains one of the most recognized commercial melodies and a favorite of popular culture trivia buffs.

Distribution

■ Alka-Seltzer is the best-selling antacid/pain reliever in the United States.

■ Alka-Seltzer is available in Alka-Seltzer Original, Alka-Seltzer Gold, Alka-Seltzer Lemon Lime, Alka-Seltzer Cherry, Alka-Seltzer Extra Strength Pain Reliever, Alka-Seltzer Caplets, Alka-Seltzer Liqui-Gel Antacid, Alka-Seltzer Anti-

Gas, and Alka-Mints in Spearmint, Tropical, and Cherry.
■ Bayer operates in 150 countries.

For More Information

Bayer Corporation Consumer Care Division, Morristown, NJ.

Arm & Hammer

Baking Soda

■ **Clean a microwave oven.** Sprinkle Arm & Hammer Baking Soda on a damp sponge, scrub, and rinse.

■ **Remove tarnish from silver.** Mix a thick paste of Arm & Hammer Baking Soda with water, apply to the silver with a damp sponge, rub, rinse, and buff dry.

■ **Clean a stainless steel sink.** Sprinkle Arm & Hammer Baking Soda on a damp sponge, scrub the sink, and rinse clean.

■ **Boost the strength of liquid laundry detergent.** Add one-half cup Arm & Hammer Baking Soda, with the usual amount of detergent, to your regular wash cycle.

■ **Clean a fiberglass bathtub or shower.** Sprinkle Arm & Hammer Baking Soda on a damp sponge, scrub, and rinse clean.

■ **Clean bathroom tile.** Sprinkle Arm & Hammer Baking Soda on a damp sponge, scrub, and rinse clean.

■ **Maintain your septic tank.** Flush one cup Arm & Hammer Baking Soda down the toilet once a week. Baking soda helps maintain proper pH and alkalinity, controlling sulfide odors.

■ **Deodorize cloth diapers.** Mix one-half cup Arm & Hammer Baking Soda in two quarts of water, and soak diapers in the solution.

■ **Deodorize a disposable diaper pail.** Sprinkle liberally with Arm & Hammer Baking Soda.

■ **Deodorize garbage disposals and sink drains.** Instead of throwing out that old box of Arm & Hammer Baking Soda that's been sitting in the refrigerator or freezer, gradually pour it down the drain and flush with water. Or better yet, pour two tablespoons Arm & Hammer Baking Soda down the garbage disposal every week.

■ **Clean a refrigerator.** Sprinkle Arm & Hammer Baking Soda on a damp sponge, scrub, and rinse clean.

■ **Deodorize a dishwasher.** Sprinkle one-half cup Arm & Hammer Baking Soda on the bottom of the dishwasher between loads.

■ **Boost the strength of dishwashing liquid.** Add two full tablespoons Arm & Hammer Baking Soda to the usual amount of detergent you use.

■ **Remove burned-on food from cookware.** Dampen area, sprinkle with Arm & Hammer Baking Soda, let soak overnight, then scrub with a sponge, rinse, and dry.

■ **Clean and deodorize a cutting board.** Sprinkle Arm & Hammer Baking Soda on a damp sponge, rub the cutting board, and rinse clean.

■ **Deodorize food containers.** Mix one-quarter cup Arm & Hammer Baking Soda with one quart water, swish food containers in the solution, let soak overnight, then rinse clean.

■ **Clean coffee and teapots.** Wash in a solution of one-quarter cup Arm & Hammer Baking Soda and one quart warm water, then rinse clean.

■ **Deodorize kitchen garbage.** Sprinkle a handful of Arm & Hammer Baking Soda in the garbage pail each time you add garbage.

■ **Deodorize carpet.** Sprinkle Arm & Hammer Baking Soda lightly over the dry carpet, let sit for fifteen minutes, then vacuum up.

■ **Deodorize a cat litter box.** Cover the bottom of the litter box with one-quarter inch Arm & Hammer Baking Soda, then add the litter.

■ **Maintain the proper alkalinity in a swimming pool.**
Add one and a half pounds of baking soda for every ten
thousand gallons of water in the pool to raise total alkalinity
by 10 ppm (parts per million), keeping the total alkalinity of
the pool within the range of 80 to 150 ppm. Maintaining a
proper level of total alkalinity minimizes changes in pH
when acidic or basic pool chemicals or contaminants enter
the water, reducing chloramine formation and the corrosivity
of water, consequently reducing eye irritation and unpleas-
ant odors while improving bactericidal effectiveness.

■ **Soothe poison ivy rash or insect bites.** Make a paste
of Arm & Hammer Baking Soda and water, and apply to the
affected area.

■ **Soothe sunburn, windburn, and prickly heat.** Dissolve one-half cup Arm & Hammer Baking Soda in a tepid
bath. Soak in the bath for fifteen minutes.

■ **Take a refreshing bath.** Dissolve one-half cup Arm &
Hammer Baking Soda in a tub of warm water for soft,
smooth-feeling skin and a relaxing bath.

■ **Brush your teeth.** Plain baking soda is a gentle abrasive
that cleans like the strongest toothpaste. Apply Arm &
Hammer Baking Soda to a damp toothbrush, brush as usual,
and rinse. Of course, Arm & Hammer Baking Soda does not
contain fluoride.

■ **Wash your mouth.** Add one teaspoon Arm & Hammer
Baking Soda to one-half glass warm water, and swish through
teeth for a refreshing mouthwash.

■ **Neutralize vomit odor.** Sprinkle Arm & Hammer Baking Soda generously to cover the stained area, let sit for an hour, then vacuum up.

■ **Soothe tired feet.** Add three tablespoons Arm & Hammer Baking Soda to a basin of warm water and soak feet in the solution.

■ **Use as a deodorant.** Dust Arm & Hammer Baking Soda under arms.

■ **Clean dirt, grime, and scuff marks from doors, stoves, laminated tabletops, linoleum floors, and tile.** Sprinkle Arm & Hammer Baking Soda on a damp sponge, wipe clean, and dry.

■ **Remove coffee or tea stains from china.** Dip a damp cloth in baking soda, gently rub the china, and rinse clean.

■ **Minimize the smell of dirty laundry.** Sprinkle some Arm & Hammer Baking Soda into your hamper or laundry bag.

■ **Deodorize a closet.** Place an open box of Arm & Hammer Baking Soda on a shelf.

■ **Deodorize garment storage bags.** Sprinkle Arm & Hammer Baking Soda into the bottom of the bags.

■ **Deodorize shoes or sneakers.** In the evening, sprinkle Arm & Hammer Baking Soda inside shoes to eliminate odors. Shake out in the morning.

■ Remove crayon marks from walls or wallpaper. Sprinkle Arm & Hammer Baking Soda on a damp sponge, scrub gently to avoid mussing the paint or wallpaper, then wipe clean.

■ Clean dirt and grime from hands. Sprinkle Arm & Hammer Baking Soda onto wet hands with liquid soap, rub vigorously, rinse, and dry.

■ Remove conditioner and styling gel buildup from hair. Wash hair once a week with a tablespoon of Arm & Hammer Baking Soda mixed with your regular shampoo; rinse thoroughly, then condition and style as usual.

■ Refresh stuffed animals. Sprinkle Arm & Hammer Baking Soda on the stuffed animals, let sit for fifteen minutes, then brush off.

■ Clean high chairs, car seats, strollers, and plastic mattress protectors. Sprinkle Arm & Hammer Baking Soda on a damp sponge, wipe clean, and dry.

■ Clean baby bottles, nipples, and bottle brushes. Soak in a solution of warm water and Arm & Hammer Baking Soda, then sterilize before use.

■ Make baby clothes smell even fresher. Add one-half cup Arm & Hammer Baking Soda to baby's laundry.

■ Boost bleach. Use one-half cup Arm & Hammer Baking Soda with your normal liquid bleach to boost the bleaching action and freshen the wash.

■ **Whiten socks and dirty clothes.** Add one-half cup Arm & Hammer Baking Soda to regular laundry detergent.

■ **Clean up pet accidents.** Apply Canada Dry Club Soda to the stain, rub it in, wait a few minutes, sponge it up, let dry thoroughly, then sprinkle on Arm & Hammer Baking Soda, allow to sit for fifteen minutes, then vacuum up.

■ **Clean chrome bumpers and hubcaps.** Sprinkle Arm & Hammer Baking Soda on a damp sponge, rub surface, and wipe clean with a dry cloth.

■ **Remove dead insects from a car or truck windshield.** Sprinkle Arm & Hammer Baking Soda on a damp sponge, clean glass, and wipe clean with a dry cloth.

■ **Deodorize carpeting in a car.** Sprinkle Arm & Hammer Baking Soda on the carpet, let sit for fifteen minutes, then vacuum up.

■ **Degrease and clean barbecue grills.** Make a paste by mixing equal parts Arm & Hammer Baking Soda and water, apply with a wire brush, wipe clean, and dry with a cloth.

Invented
1846

The Name
Sodium bicarbonate, more commonly known as bicarbonate of soda, was originally used as an ingredient in cake batter to

make cakes rise; hence the combination of the words *baking* and *soda*. The Arm & Hammer symbol was first used in the early 1860s by James A. Church, who ran a spice-and-mustard business called Vulcan Spice Mills. When Church joined his father, Dr. Austin Church, in the baking soda business in 1867, he brought with him the trademark depicting the muscular arm of Vulcan, god of fire, with steel hammer in hand about to descend on an anvil.

A Short History

In 1846, John Dwight started making baking soda in the kitchen of his Massachusetts home. In 1847, he formed John Dwight and Company with his brother-in-law, Dr. Austin Church, introducing Cow Brand as the trademark for Dwight's Saleratus (aerated salt, as baking soda was then called). Church formed Church & Company to produce the baking soda, identifying his brand as Arm & Hammer. In 1896, the descendants of the founders of these two companies consolidated their interests under the name Church & Dwight Co., Inc.

Ingredients

100 percent sodium bicarbonate

Strange Facts

■ The Arm & Hammer logo ranks among the nation's most recognized product symbols.
■ Baking soda has an almost unlimited shelf life.
■ A box of baking soda can be found in nine out of ten

refrigerators. According to the *Los Angeles Times*, "More refrigerators are likely to have baking soda than working lightbulbs."

■ Baking soda was used to clean the Statue of Liberty for the 1976 Bicentennial celebration.

■ Baking soda is the main ingredient in Alka-Seltzer.

■ Baking soda was promoted as a key ingredient in 25 percent of all toothpastes sold in 1994.

■ When mixed in cake batter and heated, baking soda releases a carbon dioxide gas that causes the cake to rise.

■ Baking soda chemically neutralizes odors by turning into a sodium salt and giving off water and carbon dioxide.

■ Baking soda cleanses by neutralizing fatty acids found in most dirt and grease.

■ Arm & Hammer Baking Soda has been used to reduce air pollution in factory smokestacks. Arm & Hammer Baking Soda, when pulverized to an appropriate particle size, is, like other sodium sorbents, one of the most effective collectors of sulfur dioxide. Injecting Arm & Hammer–brand sorbent-grade sodium bicarbonate directly into the flue gas ducts of coal-fired boiler systems desulfurizes flue gas. The baking soda reacts with sulfur dioxide to form sodium sulfate, and the cleaned flue gas exits through the stack.

■ Arm & Hammer Baking Soda has been used to increase the effectiveness of sewage treatment plants. Baking soda helps maintain proper pH and alkalinity in biological digesters, fostering trouble-free operation of both anaerobic and aerobic treatment plants. Used in maintenance doses, baking soda boosts sludge compaction, alkalinity, and methane gas production while reducing biological oxygen demand and controlling sulfide odors. Plus, it's environmentally safe.

■ Baking soda can restore lakes damaged by acid rain. In

1985, Cornell professor James Bisongi Jr. restored Wolf Pond, a virtually dead fifty-acre lake in the Adirondacks, by adding nearly twenty tons of baking soda to the water to dramatically reduce the acidity.

■ The U.S. Environmental Protection Agency and the navy's Civil Engineering Lab have jointly developed an inexpensive method of using baking soda to decontaminate soil laced with halogenated organic chemicals. The halogenated contaminates are decomposed by excavating, crushing, and screening the soil; mixing in baking soda at 10 percent of its weight; and then heating the soil to 630°F for one hour. The treated soil can then be returned to its original location.

■ Arm & Hammer Baking Soda has been used to increase the butterfat content of cow and goat milk. High-grain diets typically increase acid formation in ruminant animals, interfering with the bacteria that aid digestion. Adding baking soda to cow and goat feed increases the pH in the animals' rumina, lowering the acidity, making for a more favorable environment for the microbacteria that aid digestion, elevating the rate of feed intake, and increasing milk production and the butterfat content of the milk.

Distribution

■ Arm & Hammer Baking Soda, the only nationally distributed brand-name baking soda, can be found in virtually every household in the United States.

■ Arm & Hammer Baking Soda is available in 8-ounce, 16-ounce, 32-ounce, 64-ounce, and 10-pound boxes. It is also available in 20-ounce "Fridge-Freezer Packs" with "Spill-Proof Vents" that will prevent the baking soda from spilling if the container is knocked over in the refrigerator or freezer.

For More Information

Arm & Hammer, Division of Church & Dwight Co., Inc., 469 North Harrison Street, Princeton, NJ 08543. Or telephone 1-800-524-1328 (in New Jersey, telephone 1-800-624-2889).

Original Syrup

■ **Prolong the life of a Christmas tree.** Cut an extra inch off the bottom of the tree, stand the tree in a bucket of cold water to which one cup of Aunt Jemima Original Syrup has been added, and let the tree soak for two or three days before decorating.

■ **Condition hair and prevent split ends and frizzies.** Massage Aunt Jemima Original Syrup into dry hair, cover hair with a shower cap for thirty minutes, then shampoo and rinse thoroughly.

■ **Make maple frosting.** Combine one stick of margarine, one-third cup of Aunt Jemima Original Syrup, and three to four cups powdered sugar. Beat until desired thickness.

■ **Make a Maple Yogurt Smoothie.** In a blender, combine one cup ice cubes, one cup plain yogurt, one-half cup low-fat milk, one-third cup Aunt Jemima Original Syrup, and one peeled banana. Cover and blend on high speed until smooth and thick.

■ **Substitute syrup for sugar when cooking.** Use three-quarters cup of Aunt Jemima Original Syrup for each cup of sugar.

■ **Revive an ailing house plant.** Add two tablespoons

Aunt Jemima Original Syrup at the base of the plant once a month.

■ **Relieve a sore throat.** Take two teaspoons Aunt Jemima Original Syrup to coat and soothe the throat.

■ **Sweeten a cup of coffee or tea.** Substitute a teaspoon of Aunt Jemima Original Syrup for each teaspoon of sugar or honey.

■ **Lure insects away from an outdoor party or barbecue.** Coat a few small pieces of cardboard with Aunt Jemima Original Syrup and place around the perimeter of the yard. Stinging insects, like wasps, bees, and yellow jackets, will be attracted to the syrup instead of your guests.

Invented
1964

The Name
While seeking a name and package design for the world's first self-rising pancake mix, creator Chris L. Rutt saw a vaudeville team known as Baker

and Farrell whose act included Baker singing the catchy song "Aunt Jemima" dressed as a Southern mammy. Inspired by the wholesome name and image, Rutt appropriated them both to market his new pancake mix.

A Short History

In 1889, Chris L. Rutt, a newspaperman in St. Joseph, Missouri, began working on creating a self-rising pancake mix. Within a year, he and two associates developed the first pancake mix ever made. Unable to raise the money to promote Aunt Jemima pancake mix, Rutt and his associates sold their company to R. T. Davis Mill and Manufacturing Company, which promoted the new product at the World's Columbian Exposition in Chicago in 1893. The company hired Nancy Green, a famous African-American cook born in Montgomery County, Kentucky, to play the part of Aunt Jemima and demonstrate the pancake mix. As Aunt Jemima, Nancy Green made and served over one million pancakes by the time the fair closed, prompting buyers to place over fifty thousand orders for Aunt Jemima pancake mix. For the next thirty years, Green played the part of Aunt Jemima at expositions all over the country. In 1924, the Quaker Oats Company bought the Aunt Jemima Mills.

Ingredients

Corn syrup, sugar syrup, high-fructose corn syrup, water, maple syrup, cellulose gum, salt, artificial and natural flavors, caramel color, sodium benzoate and sorbic acid (preservatives), sodium hexametaphosphate

Strange Facts

■ A caricature of Nancy Green as a black mammy was pictured on early packages of Aunt Jemima pancake mix. In 1917, Aunt Jemima was redrawn as a smiling, heavyset black housekeeper with a bandanna wrapped around her head. In 1989, the company modernized Aunt Jemima, making her thinner, eliminating her bandanna, and giving her a perm and a pair of pearl earrings.

■ In 1923, Nancy Green died in an automobile accident at the age of eighty-nine.

■ Before Aunt Jemima pancake mix was invented, pancakes were strictly a breakfast food. The appeal and convenience of Aunt Jemima pancake mix made pancakes a standard for lunch and dinner.

■ The Boys Club of Rockford, Illinois, was built and is operated solely from funds raised annually by Rockford Kiwanians and Aunt Jemima.

■ Frank Zappa recorded an album titled *Electric Aunt Jemima*.

■ In 1994, pop singer Gladys Knight became a spokesperson for Aunt Jemima Lite Syrup.

Distribution

■ In 1994, Aunt Jemima sold over $105 million worth of syrup, accounting for 18 percent of the syrup category.

For More Information

The Quaker Oats Company, P.O. Box 049003, Chicago, IL 60604-9003. Or telephone 1-800-407-2247.

Laser Labels

■ **Label your eyeglass case.** Print your name, address, and phone number on an Avery Laser Label and adhere it inside your eyeglass case.

■ **Identify your camera.** Print your name on an Avery Laser Label and adhere it to the back of your camera so you can easily identify it at family get-togethers or parties where many people bring the same type of camera.

■ **Label Halloween candy.** Print your name, address, and phone number on Avery Laser Labels and adhere them to the wrappers of the candy you give out for Halloween, so parents will know whom the candy comes from.

■ **Label your books and compact discs.** Print your name, address, and phone number on Avery Laser Labels and adhere them to books and CDs.

■ **Label your child's school supplies.** Print your child's name on Avery Laser Labels and adhere them to rulers, crayon boxes, lunch boxes, and thermos bottles, then cover with transparent tape.

■ **Label frozen foods and leftovers.** Print information about the contents and the date you place the food in the refrigerator or freezer on Avery Laser Labels.

■ **Label computer discs.** Use Avery Laser Labels. Avery Dennison also makes diskette labels.

■ **Label storage boxes.** Label the contents of any box you put into storage or in the attic or garage with an Avery Laser Label so you can easily identify the contents.

Invented

1935

The Name

Avery Laser Labels are named after company founder R. Stanton Avery.

A Short History

In 1935, Stan Avery founded Kum-Kleen Products, making self-adhesive labels using machinery he had developed from an old washing machine motor and sewing machine. Avery renamed his company Avery Adhesives, which incorporated in 1946 and became the Avery

Adhesive Label Corporation, with 80 percent of its sales stemming from industrial labels sold to manufacturers to label their own products.

In 1952, Avery lost its patent rights for self-adhesive labels, compelling Avery to create a new division—the Avery Paper Company—to produce and market self-adhesive base materials.

In 1961, Avery went public, and grew rapidly over the next three decades, establishing new production facilities around the world, and introducing new, technologically superior adhesives. Major acquisitions extended the company's reach in office products and specialty chemicals, expanding Avery's product line and strengthening its market position. The company's primary brand names—Avery, in office products markets, and Fasson, for industrial customers—became recognized worldwide leaders in their industries.

In 1990, Avery International Corporation merged with Dennison Manufacturing Company. The merger created Avery Dennison, a substantially strengthened company with global leadership in office products, adhesives, and label converting technology.

Ingredients
Paper, adhesive

Strange Facts
■ Dennison Manufacturing, which merged with Avery International in 1990, was founded by Andrew Dennison and his son Aaron Dennison in 1844. The company made jewelry boxes, and later manufactured tags, labels, and tissue paper.

■ Avery Dennison works closely with leading software companies to incorporate preset layouts for Avery labels directly into the software. These preset layouts enable computer users to print labels almost effortlessly without the hassles of having to adjust margins, set tabs, or create tables.

■ In 1977, Avery began supplying adhesives for disposable diapers.

■ Avery Dennison makes self-adhesive postage stamps for the United States Postal Service.

Distribution

■ Avery Dennison produces a wide variety of address labels. Avery labels are available in white, clear, or fluorescent colors, and are specially designed for laser or ink jet printers. Avery labels are also available for copiers, dot matrix printers, and typewriters.

■ Avery Dennison also manufactures and markets pressure-sensitive adhesives and materials, office products, tags, retail systems, and specialty chemicals.

■ Avery Dennison makes the best-selling office address labels in the United States.

■ Avery Dennison operates two hundred manufacturing facilities and sales offices in thirty-six countries.

■ In 1996, Avery Dennison sold more than $3.2 billion worth of pressure-sensitive adhesives and materials.

For More Information

Avery Dennison Corporation, Avery Division, Consumer Service Center, P.O. Box 5244, Diamond Bar, CA 91765-4000. Or telephone 1-800-462-8379.

■ Remove spots from rugs or carpets. Squirt Barbasol on stain, scrub, and wash with water.

■ Clean upholstery. Apply Barbasol sparingly to stain and rub gently with a damp cloth.

■ Make finger paint. Let children paint with Barbasol on a kitchen table or vinyl tablecloth. For color, sprinkle in powdered tempera paint or add a drop of food coloring.

■ Clean grease from hands. Rubbing Barbasol between your hands will dissolve grime without water. Keep a can of it at the workbench.

■ Remove latex paint from hands. The emollients and moisturizers in Barbasol ease latex paint from skin.

■ Keep your bathroom mirror from fogging up. Spread Barbasol on and wipe off. Can last two to three weeks.

■ Lubricate squeaky hinges. Spray the joint with Barbasol.

■ Break in a baseball glove. Rub the center of the glove with Barbasol, place a baseball in the glove, fold the mitt around it, and secure with rubber bands. Tuck the glove under a mattress overnight.

■ **Prevent ski goggles from fogging up.** Spray the goggles with Barbasol, then wipe clean.

Invented
1920

The Name
Barbasol is a combination of the Roman word *barba* (meaning "beard," and the origin of the word *barber*) and the English word *solution*, signifying that the shaving cream is similar to the solution used by barbers. The stripes on the can evoke the familiarity of barbershop pole stripes.

A Short History
In 1920, Frank B. Shields, a former chemistry instructor at the Massachusetts Institute of Technology who had founded the Napco Corporation in Indianapolis to make vegetable glue, developed the formula for Barbasol, one of the first brushless shaving creams on the market. The white cream provided a quick, smooth shave and eliminated the drudgery

of having to lather up shaving soap in a mug with a shaving brush and then rubbing it onto the face. It immediately won the allegiance of thousands. The Barbasol factory and offices were both located in a small second-floor room in downtown Indianapolis. The tubes were filled, clipped, and packaged by hand. At the most, only thirty or forty gross made up an entire day's production schedule. By December 1920, Barbasol had outgrown the Napco Corporation and the Barbasol Company was created.

Barbasol was widely advertised on early radio by musical performers—most memorably Harry "Singin' Sam" Frankel—and by the catchy jingle "Barbasol, Barbasol . . . No brush, no lather, no rub-in . . . Wet your razor, then begin."

In 1962, Pfizer—the pharmaceutical company founded in 1849 in Brooklyn by Charles Pfizer and his cousin, confectioner Charles Erhart, to manufacture camphor, citric acid, and santonin—acquired the Barbasol line of shaving products, extending and updating the popular old brand.

Ingredients

Water, stearic acid, triethanolamine, isobutane, laureth-23, fragrance, propane, sodium lauryl sulfate

Strange Facts

■ A typical shave will cut about 20,000 to 25,000 facial hairs.
■ Company founder Frank Shields developed Barbasol especially for men with tough beards and tender skins because he had both of those shaving problems.
■ During the 1920s, Barbasol was endorsed by Knute Rockne, Florenz Ziegfeld, and other celebrities of the day.

■ The Depression had practically no effect on the Barbasol Company because shaving cream was not a luxury.

■ In the 1936 Indianapolis 500, Barbasol sponsored the Barbasol Special #12, painted to look like a tube of Barbasol Brushless Shaving Cream. The car finished 21st after crashing in the main stretch in the 119th lap of the 200-lap race. Today, Barbasol sponsors a NASCAR team.

■ Shaving in the shower wastes an average of ten to thirty-five gallons of water. To conserve water, fill the sink basin with an inch of water and vigorously rinse your razor often in the water after every second or third stroke.

■ A typical razor blade today is good for about ten shaves.

■ Among the 90 percent of males who shave, roughly 30 percent use electric razors.

■ Shaving daily with a wet razor exfoliates the beard area of the face, loosening and removing the top layer of skin cells, which is believed to help the skin retain its vitality and youthful appearance.

■ According to archaeologists, men shaved their faces as far back as the Stone Age—twenty thousand years ago. Prehistoric men shaved with clamshells, shark teeth, sharpened pieces of flint, and knives.

■ Ancient Egyptians shaved their faces and heads so the enemy had less to grab during hand-to-hand combat. Archaeologists have discovered gold and copper razors in Egyptian tombs dating back to the fourth century B.C.

■ The longest beard, according to the *Guinness Book of Records*, measured 17.5 feet in length and was presented to the Smithsonian Institute in 1967.

■ Aerosol shaving cream cans were introduced in the 1950s.

■ Shave gels, which turn to foam after being worked into the beard, were introduced in the late 1970s.

■ The first shaving creams specifically targeted to women were introduced in 1986.

■ Seventy percent of women rate clean-shaven men as sexy.

Distribution

■ Barbasol is available in Aerosol Foam (Original, Menthol, Lemon/Lime, Skin Conditioner, Sensitive Skin, and Aloe), Shave Gel (Regular, Lime, Skin Conditioner, and Sensitive Skin), and Brushless Shave Cream.

■ Barbasol accounts for 20 percent of all shaving preparations sold in the market.

■ Pfizer, which mass-produced penicillin during World War II, discovered Terramycin, and made Salk and Sabin polio vaccines in the 1950s, is today one of the world's leading pharmaceutical companies. It also makes BenGay, Desitin, Bain de Soleil, Cortizone, and Visine.

For More Information

Consumer Health Group, Pfizer Inc., 235 East 42nd Street, New York, NY 10017.

■ Get your whites whiter than white. Mix one-half cup Cascade and one gallon hot water in a plastic bucket. Soak clothing in this mixture overnight, dump the solution and clothes into the washing machine, and wash as usual. Add one-half cup Heinz White Vinegar to the rinse water.

■ Remove coffee and tea stains from glass cookware. Soak the glassware in a solution of two tablespoons Cascade to two quarts warm water.

■ Clean a thermos bottle. Fill the bottle with two tablespoons Cascade and hot water. Let sit for thirty minutes, then swish clean with a bottle brush and rinse thoroughly.

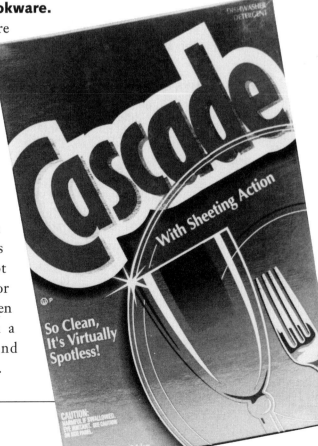

■ **Prewash stains on clothes.** Wet the fabric and sprinkle Cascade on the stain. Scrub gently with an old toothbrush, rinse, and run through the regular wash cycle.

■ **Clean dirt, grease, and grime from walls, glass, porcelain, wooden furniture, and the outsides of appliances.** Dissolve one-quarter cup Cascade in one gallon of very hot water. Scrub, then wipe clean with a dry cloth. Cascade is spot-resistant and contains water-softening agents, so everything gets shiny clean without rinsing.

■ **Whiten white polyester.** Mix one cup Cascade and one gallon warm water in a plastic bucket. Soak the clothes in this mixture overnight, then run them through the washing machine. Cascade removes the gray due to detergent residue buildup from white polyester.

■ **Clean a vase.** Place one teaspoon Cascade in a dirty glass vase, fill with water, and let sit overnight. The next morning, simply rinse clean.

■ **Clean bathtub rings.** Sprinkle Cascade on a wet sponge and scrub.

■ **Clean cooked-on oil from a popcorn popper or baked-on food from a pot or pan.** Mix a heaping tablespoon of Cascade with hot water, put it in the popper (pot or pan), and let soak overnight.

Invented

1955

The Name

The word *cascade* suggests the way the crystals cascade over the dishes to clean them.

A Short History

In the 1950s, when postwar prosperity made the automatic dishwasher popular, Procter & Gamble developed a detergent specially blended to capitalize on the new home market for these machines. In 1955, blue-green, pine-scented Cascade came in a box wrapped in gold paper, changed to green in 1958. In 1972, Procter & Gamble introduced Lemon Scent Cascade. In 1976, a new color dye was used, and the phosphate content was reduced from 12.9 to 8.3 percent in response to legislation barring high levels of phosphates. In 1983, Cascade was repackaged in a green laminated box. Cascade's phosphate content was lowered to 8.1 percent in 1989. In 1990, Cascade was reformulated without any dyes, and in 1992, the phosphate content was lowered again, to 7.5 percent.

Ingredients

Water softeners (complex sodium phosphates and sodium carbonate), cleaning agent (chlorine bleach), water spot prevention agents (nonionic surfactant), dishwasher and china protection agent (sodium silicate), processing aids (sodium sulfate), and perfume

Strange Facts

■ After World War II, complex phosphates, primarily sodium tripolyphosphate, were a key factor in the development of the first synthetic detergent.

■ Phosphates contain the element phosphorus, one of many nutrients essential to water plants and algae. Since phosphorus also contributes to accelerated eutrophication—the excessively rapid growth of aquatic plant life in water bodies—many state governments have banned the sale of detergents with phosphates.

■ Since 1976, Procter & Gamble has reduced the amount of phosphate in Cascade by more than 41 percent, adding extra surfactants to boost the cleaning power.

■ State legislatures that have banned detergents that contain phosphates have made an exception for automatic dishwasher detergents because, until recently, no automatic dishwasher detergent would work without phosphates.

Distribution

■ Cascade is the best-selling automatic dishwashing detergent in the United States.

■ Cascade is also available in Lemon (King Size and Family Size), Liquid Gel (Baking Soda Fresh Scent and Family Size), and Lemon Liquid Gel (King Size and Family Size).

For More Information

Procter & Gamble, One Procter & Gamble Plaza, Cincinnati, OH 45202. Or telephone 1-800-765-5516.

ChapStick

Lip Balm

■ **Stop bleeding while shaving.** Dab on some ChapStick if you nick yourself.

■ **Prevent car battery corrosion.** Smear ChapStick on clean car battery terminals.

■ **Lubricate a zipper.** Rub ChapStick along the teeth of the zipper to make it zip smoothly.

■ **Moisturize skin.** Rubbing ChapStick on your face protects the skin from windburn while snow skiing.

■ **Remove a ring stuck on a finger.** Coat finger with ChapStick and slide the ring off.

■ **Lubricate nails and screws.** Nails and screws rubbed with ChapStick will go into wood more easily.

■ **Groom a mustache or eyebrows.** A little ChapStick will keep the ends of a mustache waxed together and keep bushy eyebrow hairs in place.

■ **Shine leather shoes.** In a pinch, rub ChapStick over the leather and buff with a dry, clean cloth.

■ **Lubricate furniture drawers and windows.** Rub ChapStick on the casters of drawers and windows so they slide open and shut easily.

■ **Prevent hair coloring from dyeing your skin.** Rub ChapStick along your hairline before coloring your hair.

Invented
Early 1880s

The Name
ChapStick is apparently named for the fact that you can heal *chap*ped lips by applying the *stick* of balm.

A Short History
In the early 1880s, Dr. C. D. Fleet, a physician and pharmacological tinkerer who lived in Lynchburg, Virginia, invented a lip balm in the form of a wickless candle wrapped in tinfoil and called it ChapStick. The lip balm was sold locally without much success. In 1912, another Lynchburg resident, John Morton, bought the rights to ChapStick for five dollars. In the family kitchen, his wife melted the pink ChapStick mixture on her kitchen stove, poured the liquid through a small funnel into brass tubes held in a rack, and then set the rack on the porch to cool. The Mortons cut the molded ChapStick into sticks and placed them into containers for shipping.

In 1963, the A. H. Robins Company acquired ChapStick lip balm from Morton Manufacturing Corporation and, in

1971, added four flavors. In 1989, American Home Products Corporation, makers of Chef Boyardee foods and a leader in women's health care products, acquired A. H. Robins.

Ingredients

ACTIVE INGREDIENTS: 44 percent petrolatums, 1.5 percent padimate 0, 1 percent lanolin, 1 percent isopropyl myristate, 0.5 percent cetyl alcohol; INACTIVE INGREDIENTS: arachadyl propionate, camphor, carnauba wax, D&C red 6 barium lake, FD&C yellow 5 aluminum lake, fragrance, isopropyl lanolate, methylparaben, mineral oil, 2-octyl dodecanol, oleyl alcohol, polyphenylmethylsiloxane 556, propylparaben, titanium dioxide, wax paraffin, white wax

Strange Facts

■ Suzi Chaffey, a member of the United States Olympic Women's Alpine Skiing Team, became a spokesperson for ChapStick in the 1970s, using the nickname Suzi Chapstick.
■ In the 1994 movie *Clifford*, Clifford (Martin Short) substitutes lipstick for ChapStick in Martin's (Charles Grodin's) pocket, and Martin applies the lipstick shortly before giving a toast at dinner with his future in-laws.

Distribution

■ ChapStick lip balms are available in five flavors: Regular, Orange, Cherry, Strawberry, and Mint. ChapStick lip balm is also available in Medicated, Ultra SPF 30, Petroleum Jelly Plus, and Lip Moisturizer SPF 15 with Vitamin E and Aloe.
■ Whitehall-Robins Healthcare's parent company, Ameri-

can Home Products, sold $819 million worth of food products in 1995.

■American Home Products makes the estrogen drug Premarin, the most prescribed drug in America, and the contraceptive implant Norplant. The company also makes Advil, Anacin, Chef Boyardee, Crunch 'n Munch, Denorex, Gulden's, Jiffy Pop, Pam No Stick Cooking Spray, Preparation H, and Robitussin.

For More Information

Whitehall-Robins Healthcare, 1 Campus Drive, Parsippany, NJ 07054. Or telephone 1-201-660-5500.

Cover Girl

NailSlicks Classic Red

■ **Adjust the water in the bath or shower effortlessly.** Turn the bathtub or shower faucets to the temperature you prefer, then mark the faucet(s) and the wall with a dot of Cover Girl NailSlicks Classic Red so the dots can be aligned immediately every time you bathe or shower.

■ **Label golf, tennis, and squash balls.** Paint a small mark with Cover Girl NailSlicks Classic Red so you can easily identify your own sports equipment.

■ **Make the raised gradation marks on plastic baby bottles clearly visible.** Paint the gradation marks with Cover Girl NailSlicks Classic Red.

■ **Label children's toys.** Simply paint your child's name on the bottom of his or her favorite toys with Cover Girl NailSlicks Classic Red so they won't get lost.

■ **Repaint faded gradation marks on measuring cups.** Carefully repaint the gradation marks with Cover Girl NailSlicks Classic Red.

■ Label poisons and medicines. Paint an *X* with Cover Girl NailSlicks Classic Red on containers of poison and medicine bottles, and teach your children to never touch any bottle or box labeled with a red *X*.

■ Label hot water faucets for younger children. Paint the tops of the hot water faucets with Cover Girl NailSlicks Classic Red for your children's protection.

■ Locate the arrows or markings on childproof caps easily. Paint the arrows or other markings on childproof medicine bottles with Cover Girl NailSlicks Classic Red so you can line them up easier.

■ Thread a needle with ease. Dip the end of the thread into Cover Girl NailSlicks Classic Red, let dry, and thread.

■ Seal an envelope. Use Cover Girl NailSlicks Classic Red to seal a letter as you would use sealing wax.

■ Teach your child to push the red button on the phone in an emergency. Paint a red dot with Cover Girl NailSlicks Classic Red in the middle of the *0* on your telephone so young children can always call for help.

■ Readjust your thermostat quickly. Paint a dot of Cover Girl NailSlicks Classic Red to mark the temperature at which you usually set your thermostat.

■ Remind yourself to turn off your calculator or camera flash attachment. Paint the off button with Cover Girl NailSlicks Classic Red.

Invented

1977

The Name

Cover Girl has always been about models—and linking famous magazine "cover girls" with its products.

A Short History

In 1914, pharmacist Dr. George Bunting combined medication and vanishing cream in the prescription room of his Baltimore drugstore to create "Dr. Bunting's Sunburn Remedy." A customer told Bunting, "Your cream knocked my eczema," inspiring Bunting to change the name of his sunburn remedy to Noxzema. For three years, Bunting mixed, heated, and poured Noxzema from a large coffee pot into blue jars—ultimately founding the Noxzema Chemical Company in 1917. With the backing of Bunting's fellow druggists, Noxzema achieved national distribution in 1938.

In 1961, Noxzema launched the Cover Girl line of cosmetics with an advertising campaign using famous and fashionable cover girls raving over the new makeup. In 1966, the company changed its name to the Noxell Corporation. In 1989, Procter & Gamble Cosmetics and Fragrances bought Noxell.

Ingredients

Ethyl acetate, butyl acetate, nitrocellulose, propyl acetate, tosylamide/epoxy resin, dibutyl phthalate, isopropyl alcohol, stearalkonium bentonite, stearalkonium hectorite, camphor, benzophenone-1; MAY CONTAIN: Titanium dioxide, guanine, red 6 barium lake. iron oxides, red #7 calcium lake, yellow #5 aluminum lake, red #34 calcium lake, ferric ammonium ferrocyanide, mica, bismuth, oxychloride

Strange Facts

■ In 3000 B.C., Chinese artists combined gum arabic, egg white, gelatin, and beeswax to create varnishes, enamels, and lacquers—which Chinese aristocrats started applying to their fingernails as a status symbol.

■ The cosmetics industry in the United States includes face makeup (representing 35 percent of sales in 1992), eye cosmetics (30 percent), lip products (23 percent), and nail products (12 percent).

Distribution

■ In the United States, Cover Girl is the number-one cosmetics company, followed by number-two Revlon and number-three Maybelline.

For More Information

Procter & Gamble Cosmetics and Fragrances, 11050 York Road, Hunt Valley, MD 21030. Or telephone 1-888-COVER-GIRL, a toll-free number featuring live operators who offer consumers "mini-makeovers" and product information.

All-Vegetable Shortening

■**Prevent diaper rash.** Use Crisco All-Vegetable Shortening as a balm on a baby's behind.

■**Prevent snow from sticking to a shovel.** Lubricate the shovel with Crisco All-Vegetable Shortening before you start shoveling.

■**Clean grease and dirt from hands.** Rub in Crisco All-Vegetable Shortening before using soap.

■**Make white clown makeup.** Mix two tablespoons Kingsford's Corn Starch with one tablespoon Crisco All-Vegetable Shortening. For colored makeup, add a few drops of food coloring.

■**Remove lipstick from clothes.** Rub in a dab of Crisco All-Vegetable Shortening, then rinse the stained area with Canada Dry Club Soda.

■**Season new cast-iron cookware.** Apply a thin coating of solid, unsalted Crisco All-Vegetable Shortening, and bake in an oven at 200°F for two hours. Repeat this procedure after the first few times of use.

■**Revitalize wooden salad bowls.** Rub with Crisco All-Vegetable Shortening inside and out, let sit overnight, then remove excess with paper towels.

■**Clean ink from hands and vinyl surfaces.** Apply Crisco All-Vegetable Shortening and wipe clean.

■**Preserve a wooden cutting board.** Rub with Crisco All-Vegetable Shortening, let sit overnight, then remove excess with paper towels.

■**Polish rubber galoshes.** Rub on Crisco All-Vegetable Shortening.

■**Remove homemade candles from molds easily.** Apply a thin coat of Crisco All-Vegetable Shortening to the inside of the candle mold before pouring in the hot wax.

■**Remove tar from clothing.** Scrape off as much tar as possible, place a lump of Crisco All-Vegetable Shortening over the spot, wait three hours, then wash.

Invented

1911

The Name

The two suggested names for the vegetable shortening—
Krispo (the word *crisp* combined with the then-popular suffix
-o) and Cryst (an onomatopoeia for the hissing and crackling
sound foods make while being fried)—were combined to
form the unique hybrid Crisco.

A Short History

In 1837, candlemaker William Procter and soapmaker James
Gamble merged their small Cincinnati businesses, creating
Procter & Gamble. By 1859, P&G had become one of the
largest companies in Cincinnati, with sales of $1 million. In
1879, the company introduced Ivory, a floating soap. Procter
& Gamble introduced Crisco, the first mass-marketed, 100
percent vegetable shortening, in 1911.

The first cans of Crisco came with an eight-page circular
cookbook cut to fit the lid. Starting in 1913, Procter &
Gamble sent six home economists across the country to give
week-long demonstrations (advertised as "cooking schools")
to show homemakers how to get better results by using
Crisco in their cooking. After the demonstrations, the home
economists would hand out souvenir baskets of various food
samples, one-and-a-half-pound cans of Crisco, and special
Crisco cookbooks to the eager audiences.

Ingredients

Partially hydrogenated soybean and cottonseed oils, mono- and diglycerides

Strange Facts

■ The first Crisco cookbook, printed in 1911 and titled "Tested Crisco Recipes," has been followed through the years by more than sixty Crisco cookbooks.

■ Cooking experts from the *Ladies' Home Journal* and other women's magazines worked out Crisco's early cookbooks and tested the recipes in their magazines' kitchens. In 1923, Procter & Gamble set up its own kitchen in Cincinnati to create and test recipes.

■ Procter & Gamble's first three radio network programs in 1923 consisted entirely of cake and cookie recipes for Crisco.

■ Criso All-Vegetable Shortening will easily glide out of a bowl or measuring cup that was previously used to beat or measure eggs.

■ Procter & Gamble advertising innovations included sponsorship of daytime dramas, the first being *The Puddle Family*, a 1932 radio show.

■ Although Crisco appears solid, it actually contains over 80 percent liquid oil. The oil is suspended in a lattice of fat solids much like honey is held in a honeycomb.

Distribution

■ Procter & Gamble also makes Tide, Spic and Span, Duncan Hines, Charmin, Folgers, Crest, Head & Shoulders, Pampers, Nyquil, Noxzema, Jif, Max Factor, Pringles, Hawaiian

Punch, Bounce, Cascade, Cheer, Comet, Downy, Joy, Mr. Clean, Chloraseptic, Clearasil, Cover Girl, Ivory, Luvs, Metamucil, Oil of Olay, Pepto-Bismol, Scope, Secret, Vicks, Vidal Sassoon, and Zest.

For More Information

Procter & Gamble, Box 5558, Cincinnati, OH 45201. Or telephone 1-800-543-7276.

Dixie Cups

■ **Protect tomatoes from cutworms and insects.**
Remove the bottoms of Dixie Cups and push the cups into
the soil to encircle young plants.

■ **Improvise a funnel.** Punch a hole in the bottom of a Dixie Cup near the edge.

■ **Make a weather vane.** Remove the bottom from a Dixie Cup and hang the cup horizontally from a string. The opening will tend to face into the wind.

■ **Make a poor man's telephone.** Punch a small hole in the bottom of two Dixie Cups. Then thread the ends of a long piece of string through the holes and tie each end to a button. You and a friend each take a cup and walk apart until the string is straight and taut. Speak into the open end of your cup. Your sound waves travel along the string and can be heard by your friend through the open end of the other cup.

■ **Germinate seeds.** Turn a Dixie cup upside down and use a pencil to poke a hole in the center of the bottom. Then fill half of the cup with soil. Place seed inside and cover with more soil. Follow directions on seed package for proper care. Write plant name on cup with marker.

■ **Turn soap slivers into liquid soap.** Place slivers of soap in a Dixie Cup with a little water, then wait a few days.

■ **Make a Strawberry Short Cup.** Place a spoonful of whipped topping in the bottom of six nine-ounce Dixie Cups. Alternate filling the cups with strawberries and cubed cake to one inch below the rim. Press down with a spoon to fill any air pockets. Complete with whipped topping and a single whole strawberry. Serves six.

■ **Relieve an earache caused by the change in pressure in an airplane.** Dampen a paper towel with hot water, ball it up, and place in the bottom of a Dixie Cup. Then hold the Dixie Cup over your ear. The steam from the hot water will soften the wax in your ear, alleviating the pain.

■ **Make an anemometer to determine wind speeds.** Using a hole puncher, punch one hole in four Dixie Cups, about a half inch below the rim. Then take a fifth Dixie Cup and punch four equally spaced holes about a quarter inch below the rim and a fifth hole in the center of the bottom of the cup. Push a straight plastic drinking straw through the hole in one of four cups. When it hits the inside of the cup across from the hole, fold the end of the straw, and staple it to the side of the cup. Slide the free end of the straw through two opposite holes in the fifth cup with the four holes. Then push the free end of the straw through the hole in a second one-hole Dixie Cup. Fold the end of the straw and staple it to the inside of the cup across from the hole, making certain the cup faces in the opposite direction from the first cup. Repeat this procedure using the remaining two cups and a second straight plastic straw, aligning the four cups so that their open ends face in the same direction around the center cup. Push the eraser end of a sharpened pencil through the bottom hole in the center cup, then push a pin through the two straws where they intersect and into the end of the pencil eraser as far as it will go.

To find the wind speed, multiply the number of revolutions per minute by the circumference of the circle (in feet) made by the revolving paper cups. The result is the speed of the wind in feet per minute.

Invented

1908

The Name

Inventor Hugh Moore's paper cup factory was located next door to the Dixie Doll Company in the same downtown loft building. The word *Dixie* printed on the company's door reminded Moore of the story he had heard as a boy about "dixies," the ten-dollar banknotes printed with the French word *dix* in big letters across the face of the bill. They had been issued in the early 1800s by a New Orleans bank renowned for its strong currency. The "dixies," Moore decided, had the qualities he wanted people to associate with his paper cups, and with permission from his neighbor, he used the name.

A Short History

In 1908, Hugh Moore started the American Water Supply Company of New England to market a vending machine that for one penny would dispense a cool drink of water in an individual, clean, disposable paper cup. Moore soon realized that his sanitary cups had greater sales potential than his water, particularly when Dr. Samuel Crumbine, a health official in Dodge City, Kansas, began crusading for a law to ban the public tin dipper. Lacking the capital to manufacture enough paper cups to abolish the tin dipper, Moore and his associate Lawrence Luellen traveled to New York City with a few handmade samples and eventually hooked up with an investment banker who invested $200,000 in the venture, incorporated as the Public Cup Vendor Company in 1909.

That same year, Kansas passed the first state law abolishing the public dipper and Professor Alvin Davison of Lafayette College published a study reporting that germs of communicable diseases could be found on public dipping tins. As state after state outlawed public tins, Moore and his associates created a paper cup dispenser to be distributed for free to businesses and schools who would the buy the paper cups. By 1910 the company had changed its name to the Individual Drinking Cup Company, only to change it again in 1912 to

Health Kups and yet again in 1919 to Dixie Cups. In 1923, Dixie Cups produced a two-and-a-half-ounce Dixie Cup for ice cream, giving the ice cream industry a way to sell individual servings of ice cream and compete with bottled soft drinks and candy bars. The American Can Company purchased Dixie Cups and merged the company with Northern Paper. In 1982, the James River Corporation acquired Dixie Cups/Northern Paper for $455 million.

Ingredients

Paper, wax

Strange Facts

■ Etymologists believe that the sobriquet for the southern United States, Dixie Land, originated on the Mississippi River before the Civil War with riverboat men for whom a "dixie" was a New Orleans banknote printed with the word *dix*, French for "ten."

■ The Dixie Cups, a popular singing trio comprised of sisters Nadine, Marta, and Lucile LeCupsa, sang the 1964 hit song "Chapel of Love."

■ While playing telephone operator Ernestine on *Saturday Night Live*, Lily Tomlin said, "Next time you complain about your phone service, why don't you try using two Dixie Cups with a string?"

Distribution

■ Dixie holds the number-one spot in commercial food service, ahead of Sweetheart Cups.

- Dixie also manufactures paper plates.
- Dixie Cups are available in a wide range of designs.

For More Information

James River Corporation, Consumer Products–Dixie, Norwalk, CT 06856-6000. Or telephone 1-800-243-5384.

■ Keep ski goggles from fogging up. Spray the inside of the lens with Endust, then wipe clean.

■ Polish leather shoes. Spray Endust on shoes and shine with a cloth.

■ Oil a squeaky door. Lubricate the hinges with Endust.

■ Prevent stains on kitchen drainboards. Coat rubber drainboard trays with a light application of Endust.

■ Sweep up dust and dirt with ease. Spray the bristles of your broom or mop with Endust before sweeping.

■ Prevent water spots and soap scum on shower walls and doors. Coat the tile walls with Endust and wipe clean.

■ Make cleaning grease splatters on the wall behind the stove easier. Spray the clean, painted wall behind your stove with a generous coat of Endust and buff well. Future grease spatters can be wiped away with a dry sheet of Bounty.

■ Revitalize dull candles. Spray Endust on a cloth and wipe the candles thoroughly.

■ **Clean brass.** Use very fine steel wool sprayed with Endust.

Invented
1956

The Name
The word *endust* is a clever combination of the words *end* and *dust*, signifying what this wonderful furniture spray does, when used with a dust cloth.

A Short History
The Drackett Company of Cincinnati, makers of such products as Windex, introduced Endust in 1956. In 1993, Kiwi Brands acquired both Endust and Behold.

Ingredients
Oils, cleaning agents, fragrance

Strange Facts
■ Endust contains no wax or silicone.

Distribution

■ Endust is available in Regular, Lemon, and Country Harvest.

■ Kiwi Brands also makes Kiwi shoe care products, Ty-D-Bol toilet cleaner, and Behold furniture polish.

■ Kiwi Brand's parent company, Sara Lee, makes Bali intimate apparel, Champion activewear, Coach leather goods, Hanes hosiery and apparel, L'eggs panty hose, Playtex intimate apparel, and Ball Park frankfurters.

For More Information

Kiwi Brands, Douglasville, PA 19518-1239. Or telephone 1-800-392-7733.

Toothpicks

■ **Apply glue.** Dip one end of a Forster Toothpick into the glue to apply small drops.

■ **Improvise a bookmark.** Keep your place with a Forster Toothpick.

■ **Plug small nail or thumb-tack holes in wood.** Dip the end of a Forster Toothpick in glue, insert into the hole, slice flush with a single-edge razor blade, sand smooth, and refinish the wood.

■ **Decorate a cake with ease.** Use a Forster Toothpick to draw your design on the cake, then squeeze the frosting over your lines.

■ **Paint small crevices or repair scratches in furniture.** Dip a Forster Toothpick in paint to retouch fine scratches or reach small nooks and crannies.

■ **Root a potato or avocado.** Securely insert four Forster Toothpicks equidistantly around the equator of the potato or avocado. (You can use a nail to punch starter holes in the avocado.) Fill a glass with water, set the potato or avocado in the glass so the toothpicks allow only the bottom half of the potato or avocado to sit in the water. Place the glass on a window ledge to get sunlight. When roots and shoots appear, pot the plant in soil.

■ **Repair broken eyeglasses temporarily.** If you lose a screw from your eyeglasses, substitute a Forster Toothpick until you can get the glasses fixed properly.

■ **Mark the starting point of a roll of masking tape or packaging tape.** Stick a Forster Toothpick under the loose end of the tape so you can find the end easily the next time you use the tape.

■ **Clean tight crevices.** Dip a Forster Toothpick in alcohol to clean tight spaces.

■ **Make a garlic clove easy to handle.** Stick a Forster Toothpick into a clove of garlic before tossing it into a marinade, so you can remove it easily.

■ **Give a broken plant stem first aid.** Make a splint with a Forster Toothpick and Scotch Tape.

■ **Identify rare, medium, and well-done steaks on your barbecue grill.** Use colored Forster Toothpicks to mark steaks on the barbecue.

■ **Cook sausages with ease.** Use two Forster Toothpicks to skewer two or three sausages together to make them easier to turn and brown evenly.

■ **Tighten a loose screw.** Insert a Forster Toothpick into the screw hole, break it off at the surface, and rescrew the screw.

■ **Push fabrics through the pressure foot of a sewing machine.** Use a Forster Toothpick to free fabric that gets stuck under the pressure foot.

■ **Determine whether a cake is baked.** Insert a Forster Toothpick in the center of the cake and remove. If it comes out clean, the cake is ready.

■ **Clean a dog brush.** Run a Forster Toothpick through the rows of bristles.

■ **Repair a pinhole in a garden hose temporarily.** Insert a Forster Toothpick into the hole, snap it off flush with the hose's outer skin, then wrap Scotch Mailing Tape around the spot. The wooden toothpick will absorb water, swelling to seal the hole.

Invented
1887

The Name
Forster is named after company founder Charles Forster. The toothpick was named for the purpose of the small piece of wood—to remove food particles from between the teeth.

A Short History
In 1887, Charles Forster began the first wooden toothpick factory in the United States.

Ingredients
White birch

Strange Fact
■In November 1993, Leland's, a premier auctioneer of sports memorabilia, auctioned off Tom Seaver's chewed-up toothpick for $440.

Distribution
■Forster Toothpicks are the best-selling toothpicks in the United States.

For More Information
Forster Manufacturing Company, Inc., P.O. Box 657, Wilton, ME 04294. Or telephone 1-207-645-2574.

■ Hold a paper plate. Fit a paper plate inside an upside-down Frisbee during a picnic.

■ Improvise a bowl. In an emergency, an upside-down Frisbee can be used as a bowl or plate.

■ Make a birdbath. Punch three equidistant holes along the circumference of the Frisbee, insert wire, and hang the Frisbee upside-down from a tree or post. Fill with water, or let the rain do it naturally.

■ Improvise a pet dish. When camping or hiking, an upside-down Frisbee works well as a food or water dish for your dog.

■ Improvise a cookie tray. Turn the Frisbee upside-down and fill with cookies.

■ **Play Frisbee golf.** Designate a tee-off spot and choose a tree, pole, or other landmark as the "hole." Toss a Frisbee toward the "hole," pick it up wherever it lands, and continue tossing until you hit the "hole." Keep score. The player with the fewest tosses to hit all the holes wins.

Invented
1957

The Name
Frisbee was inspired by the *Frisbie* Pie Company of Bridgeport, Connecticut, founded by William Russell Frisbie.

A Short History
In the 1870s, William Russell Frisbie opened a bakery called the Frisbie Pie Company in Bridgeport, Connecticut. His lightweight pie tins were embossed with the family name. In the mid-1940s, students at Yale University tossed the empty pie tins as a game. In the 1950s, Walter Frederick Morrison, a Los Angeles building inspector determined to capitalize on Hollywood's obsession with UFOs, designed a lightweight plastic disc based on the Frisbie bakery's pie tins, but changed the name to Flyin' Saucer to avoid legal hassles. Morrison sold the rights to the Wham-O Manufacturing Co. of San Gabriel, California, and on January 13, 1957, Americans were introduced to the Frisbee. The Frisbie Pie Company went out of business in 1958. In 1994, Mattel acquired Wham-O.

Ingredients

Polyurethane

Strange Fact

■ In May 1989, to commemorate the alleged fiftieth anniversary of the Frisbee, Middlebury College in Vermont unveiled a bronze statue of a dog jumping to catch a Frisbee. According to Middlebury legend, five undergraduates driving through Nebraska in 1939 suffered a flat tire. As two boys changed the tire, a third found a discarded pie tin from the Frisbie Pie Company near a cornfield and threw the circular disc into the air. Middlebury President Olin Robison told *Time* magazine, "Our version of the story is that it happened all over America, but it started here."

Distribution

■ In the United States, more Frisbee discs are sold each year than baseballs, basketballs, and footballs combined.

For More Information

■ Mattel, Inc., 333 Continental Boulevard, El Segundo, CA 90245. Or telephone 1-800-580-9786.
■ Ultimate Players Association, P.O. Box 2331, Silver City, NM 88062.

Flexible Straws

■ **Unclog a freshly opened ketchup bottle.** Insert a GLAD Flexible Straw all the way into the bottle to add air and start the ketchup flowing.

■ **Blow bubbles.** Cut the end of a GLAD Flexible Straw diagonally, dip into bubble soap, and blow.

■ **Prevent strings on pull toys from getting tangled.** Run the string through one or more GLAD Flexible Straws and knot it at the end.

■ **Extend the spout of an oil can.** Put a GLAD Flexible Straw over the end of the spout of an oil can to reach tight spots.

■ **Prevent tangles in fine chain jewelry.** Run the chain through a length of GLAD Flexible Straw and fasten the catch.

■ **String plastic straw necklaces.** Let the kids cut up GLAD Flexible Straws instead of macaroni, and run a string of yarn through the straws to make necklaces.

■ **Elongate flower stems that are too short for a vase.** Insert the flower stems into GLAD Flexible Straws cut to whatever length you need.

■ Make croquet wickets visible on the lawn. Run the wickets through GLAD Flexible Straws before sticking them into the ground.

■ Improvise an eyedropper. Insert a GLAD Flexible Straw into the liquid, cover the open end of the straw with your finger, and lift. The liquid will stay in the straw until you release your finger.

■ Mark a stitch when knitting. Cut a one-eighth-inch length from a GLAD Flexible Straw and use as a ring to mark a stitch on needles up to size ten.

Invented
Early 1960s

The Name
GLAD apparently signifies the joy consumers will experience when using these convenient flexible straws.

A Short History
In 1917, the National Carbon Company, maker of carbon for streetlights and owner of the

Eveready trademark, merged with Union Carbide, manufacturer of calcium carbide—along with Linde Air Products (oxygen), Prest-O-Lite (calcium carbide), and Electro Metallurgical (metals)—to form Union Carbide & Carbon Corporation. In 1920, the company established its own chemicals division, which developed ethylene glycol (antifreeze), eventually marketed as Prestone. In 1957, the company changed its name to Union Carbide Corporation, and in the early 1960s it introduced GLAD plastic household products. In 1985, Union Carbide sold its line of GLAD garbage bags to First Brands Corporation. In 1986, following a catastrophic gas leak in Bhopal, India, and a hostile takeover attempt, Union Carbide put its two consumer products divisions up for sale to raise sorely needed cash. Alfred Dudley, now chairman of First Brands, led other Union Carbide executives in acquiring the company in a leveraged buyout. In 1988, First Brands went public.

Ingredient
Plastic

Strange Facts
■ The Man from GLAD, seen in television commercials during the 1970s, was a take-off on *The Man from U.N.C.L.E.*
■ In 1984, a tank at Union Carbide's pesticide plant in Bhopal, India, leaked five tons of poisonous methyl isocyanate gas, killing more than three thousand people and permanently injuring fifty thousand people. It was the world's worst industrial accident in recorded history, resulting in a $470 million settlement in India's Supreme Court in 1989.

■In 1989, the Federal Trade Commission made the First Brands Corporation end its claims that GLAD bags were biodegradable; the bags decomposed in sunlight but not underground in municipal landfills.

Distribution

■In 1995, First Brands Corporation sold over $646 million worth of plastic wrap, plastic bags, and related products.

■First Brands Corporation markets the GLAD and GLAD-Lock brands of plastic wrap, sandwich bags, and trash bags; Ever Clean, Jonny Cat, and Scoop Away cat litters; and Simonize and STP car-care products.

■First Brands's principal U.S. manufacturing plants are in Arkansas, California, Georgia, Illinois, Kansas, Mississippi, New Jersey, Ohio, Vermont, and Virginia. The company also has manufacturing plants in Canada, China, Hong Kong, the Philippines, and South Africa.

For More Information

First Brands Corporation, P.O. Box 1999, Danbury, CT 06813-1999. Or telephone 1-800-726-1001.

Parakeet Seed

■ **Substitute for rice at weddings.** Instead of throwing rice, which is difficult to clean up, give your guests packets of Hartz Parakeet Seed instead. When the wedding is over and the guests have all gone home, the birds and squirrels will clean up the birdseed.

■ **Make a bird feeder.** Punch a hole in the top of an empty cardboard tube (from a used roll of toilet paper or paper towels). Roll the cardboard tube in honey, then roll the honey-coated tube in the Hartz Parakeet Seed. Hang the birdseed-coated tube outdoors.

■ **Make artwork.** Paint a design in Elmer's Glue-All on construction paper, then cover the glue with Hartz Parakeet Seed and let dry.

Invented
1926

The Name
Company founder Max Stern named the Hartz Mountain Corporation after the Harz Mountains of Germany, his native country.

A Short History

In 1926, German immigrant Max Stern arrived in New York Harbor with his prized singing canaries and the idea of marketing live pets and pet-care products. The company soon branched out beyond birds to dogs, cats, fish, hamsters, and gerbils. Still family-owned, the Hartz Mountain Corporation is headed today by Edward Stern, grandson of Max Stern.

Ingredients

Millet seed, oat groats, canary grass seed, iodized salt

Strange Facts

■ The Harz Mountains were immortalized in Johann Goethe's poetic drama *Faust*.

■ Hartz formulated the first antibiotic birdseed, followed by the first vitamin-impregnated birdseed.

■ Arthur Godfrey started in radio as a banjo player sponsored by a birdseed company on a station in Baltimore.

■ As a boy, Steven Spielberg kept parakeets in his bedroom,

HARTZ
PARAKEET
SEED

Wholesome
and
Nutritious

FRESHNESS
GUARANTEED

Net Wt. 17 oz 481 g

flying free. Recalled his mother, Leah, in *Time* magazine: "There would be birds flying around and birdseed all over the floor. I'd just reach in to get the dirty clothes."

■ You can tell the sex of an adult budgie parakeet by the color of the skin just above the beak. On males the color is bluish, while on females the color is brownish.

■ On an episode of *Gilligan's Island*, the Skipper announces, "Everything grows from seeds."

"Not everything," objects Gilligan.

"Yes, everything," insists the Skipper. "Orange trees grow from orange seeds, apple trees grow from apple seeds, and watermelons grow from watermelon seeds."

"Yeah, but birds don't grow from birdseed," replies Gilligan.

Distribution

■ Hartz Parakeet Seed is the best-selling parakeet seed in the United States.

■ Hartz markets more than one thousand pet-care products distributed to more than forty thousand retail outlets worldwide.

■ In addition to bird foods and accessories, Hartz also makes the hugely successful Hartz 2in1® flea and tick collar.

For More Information

Hartz Mountain Corporation, Secaucus, NJ 07094. Or telephone 1-201-271-4800.

Huggies

Baby Wipes

■ **Blot up spilled coffee from a rug or carpet.** Huggies baby wipes absorb coffee without leaving a stain.

■ **Use as toilet paper after an episiotomy.** Huggies baby wipes are gentle enough for a baby and perfect after an operation on the more sensitive areas of your body.

■ **Soothe hemorrhoids.** Use Huggies baby wipes as toilet paper to avoid aggravating sensitive hemorrhoids.

■ **Clean hands after pumping gas or changing engine oil.** Keep a box of Huggies baby wipes in the trunk of the car.

- **Store game pieces.** Store loose dice, cards, playing pieces, and small toys in an empty Huggies baby wipes box.

- **Store crayons.** Keep crayons in an empty Huggies baby wipes box.

- **Store screws, nuts, and bolts.** Use empty Huggies baby wipes boxes in the workshop to hold loose screws, bolts, nuts, nails, drill bits, and spare parts.

- **Store crafts.** Organize ribbons, beads, glues, and string in empty Huggies baby wipes boxes.

- **Clean scrapes and bruises.** Huggies baby wipes are great for cleaning minor abrasions.

- **Clean shoes.** Simply wipe the shoes with a Huggies baby wipe.

Invented
1990

The Name
Huggies describes the way these disposable diapers ideally *hug* an infant's bottom without leaking. Baby Wipes obviously refers to the cloth used to *wipe* a *baby*'s bottom.

A Short History

In 1872, John Kimberly, Charles Clark, Havilah Babcock, and Frank Shattuck founded Kimberly, Clark & Company in Neenah, Wisconsin, to manufacture newsprint from rags. In 1889, the company built a pulp-and-paper plant on the Fox River and, in 1914, developed Cellucotton, a cotton substitute used by the U.S. army as surgical cotton during World War I. Army nurses used Cellucotton pads as disposable sanitary napkins, and in 1920 the company introduced Kotex, the first disposable feminine hygiene product, followed by Kleenex, the first throw-away handkerchief, in 1924. Kotex and Kleenex became household words, and in 1928, Kimberly-Clark went public on the New York Stock Exchange. In 1971, Kimberly-Clark entered the disposable diaper market, starting with Kimbies and followed by Huggies in 1978 and Huggies Pull-Ups training pants in 1989.

In 1990, the company introduced Huggies baby wipes with 80 wipes per box. In 1995, the company changed the embossing pattern on Baby Wipes and gave the wipes a scalloped edge to make it easier to grab an individual Baby Wipe from the box. Later that year, Huggies added a resealable refill pack with 160 wipes.

Ingredients

IN PICTURED PRODUCT: Purified water, propylene glycol, PEG-75 lanolin, disodium, cocoamphdiacetate, polysorbate 20, cetyl hydroxyetheylcellulose, DMDM hydantoin, methylparaben, malic acid, fragrance

Strange Facts

■ The town of Kimberly, Wisconsin, founded as a result of the Kimberly-Clark plant, was named in John Kimberly's honor.

■ During Operation Bring Hope in Somalia, U.S. troops bartered for Huggies because the disposable diapers, when moistened, provide a refreshing rubdown, almost as good as a bath.

Distribution

■ Huggies baby wipes are available in Regular (scented and unscented), Natural Care (scented and unscented), and Sensitive Skin.

■ Huggies baby wipes, Kleenex tissue, and Huggies disposable diapers are the best-selling brands of those products in the United States.

■ Kimberly-Clark sells its products in 150 countries.

■ Aside from Huggies baby wipes, Kimberly-Clark markets Kleenex tissues, Huggies diapers, Pull-Ups training pants, Kotex and Lightdays feminine products, Depend and Poise incontinence products, Cottonelle bathroom tissue, and Viva paper towels.

For More Information

Kimberly-Clark Corporation, P.O. Box 2020, Neenah, WI 54957-2020. Or telephone 1-800-558-9177.

Gelatin

■ **Style your hair.** A teaspoon of Jell-O dissolved in a cup of warm water makes an inexpensive setting lotion. Or use prepared Jell-O as you would any hair gel product.

■ **Make marshmallows.** Gelatin is the main ingredient in any recipe for marshmallows.

■ **Make wine Jell-O.** *The Joy of Cooking* suggests boiling one cup water, mixing with gelatin powder in a bowl until dissolved, then adding one cup red wine. Stir well, then refrigerate for four hours or until mixture gels. Serves four.

■ **Wrestle in Jell-O.** Pour 2,347 boxes of Jell-O into an eight-foot-square padded box, add boiling water, and chill for two days.

■ **Watch seedlings grow roots.** For a great science experiment for children, grow seeds in Jell-O and observe the root structures.

Invented

1897

The Name

May Davis Wait, the inventor's wife, came up with a name for the fruit-flavored gelatin by apparently combining the word *jelly* with *-o*, a popular suffix added to the end of a slew of food products at the time.

A Short History

In 1845, Peter Cooper, inventor of the Tom Thumb locomotive, patented the first clear powdered gelatin mix. Fifty years later, in Le Roy, New York, Pearl B. Wait, a carpenter who had been manufacturing cough medicine and laxative tea in his spare time, began experimenting with Cooper's clear gelatin, adding ingredients until he concocted a fruit flavor.

In 1899, unable to properly market his new packaged food, Wait sold his formula to Orator Francis Woodward, proprietor of the Genesee Pure Food Company. Woodward couldn't find a market for Jell-O either, until 1900, when he spent $336 to place an advertisement in the *Ladies' Home Journal*. In 1902, Woodward launched the first advertising campaign for Jell-O, proclaiming it "America's Most Famous Dessert" and introducing the charming little Jell-O Girl in 1904. By 1906, sales topped $1 million.

Ingredients

Sugar, gelatin, adipic acid (for tartness), disodium phosphate (controls acidity), fumaric acid (for tartness), red 40, artificial flavor, blue 1

Strange Facts

■ Gelatin, a colorless protein derived from the collagen contained in animal skin, tendons, and bone, is extracted by treating hides and bone with lime or acid. The material is then boiled, filtered, concentrated, dried, and ground into granules that dissolve in hot water and congeal into a gel when the solution cools.

■ As a food supplement, gelatin supplies the body with several amino acids lacking in wheat, barley, and oats.

■ Norman Rockwell illustrated two early Jell-O advertisements and recipe books.

■ According to the 1993 *Guinness Book of Records*, the world record for the largest single amount of Jell-O is held by Paul Squire and Geoff Ross, who made 7,700 gallons of watermelon-flavored pink Jell-O in a tank supplied by Pool Fab on February 5, 1981, at Roma Street Forum in Brisbane, Australia.

■ In July 1950, the FBI arrested thirty-two-year-old electrical engineer Julius Rosenberg as a spy for the Soviet Union. According to the FBI, Rosenberg had torn a Jell-O box top in half, given a piece to his brother-in-law, David Greenglass, and told him that his contact at Los Alamos would produce the other half. The contact turned out to be spy courier Harry Gold, who received atomic energy data from Greenglass and paid him $500, allegedly giving the Soviet Union the secret of the atomic bomb. Although Rosenberg insisted on his innocence, he and his wife, Ethel, were sentenced to death in 1951, and after several appeals, in June 1953, the Rosenbergs became the first Americans ever executed for using Jell-O.

■ Every April Fool's Day in Eugene, Oregon, the Maude Kerns Art Gallery holds the Jell-O Art Show, better known as "Jell-O-Rama," featuring works of local artists using Jell-O as a medium.

Distribution

■ Jell-O is the best-selling gelatin in the United States.

■ A box of Jell-O can be found in three out of four American pantries.

■ Americans eat more than 690,000 boxes of Jell-O on an average day.

■ Jell-O and Jell-O Sugar Free are available in twenty flavors, including cherry, strawberry, raspberry, lemon, lime, mango, apricot, orange, grape, peach, blackberry, berry blue, strawberry banana, wild strawberry, triple berry, and watermelon.

For More Information

Kraft Foods, Inc., Box JOGS-C, White Plains, NY 10625. Or telephone 1-800-431-1001.

Shoe Polish

■ **Stain wood.** Apply Kiwi Shoe Polish with a dry cloth.

■ **Retouch walls.** Touch up scratches, scuff marks, and holes from picture hooks with a dab of the appropriate color Kiwi Shoe Polish.

■ **Repair furniture finishes.** Cover up small scratches or discolorations on furniture or woodwork.

■ **Use as oil paint on canvas.** Some artists use Kiwi Shoe Polish as paint in oil paintings.

Invented
1906

The Name
Inventor William Ramsay named the shoe polish Kiwi in honor of his wife, Annie Elizabeth Meek Ramsay, a native of Oamaru, New Zealand. The kiwi is the national bird of New Zealand, and "Kiwi" is a common nickname for a New Zealander, just as "Yankee" is a nickname for a citizen of the United States.

A Short History

In 1906, William Ramsay invented Kiwi Boot Polish and began marketing it in Melbourne, Australia. Ramsey would load boxes of his boot polish on his horse and wagon and sell the product to ranchers to protect their boots. During World War I and World War II, Kiwi Shoe Polish's popularity spread throughout the British Commonwealth and into the United States. A few years after World War II, the Australian company opened a manufacturing plant in Philadelphia, making only black, brown, and neutral shoe polish in tins.

In 1984, Consolidated Foods purchased Kiwi. The following year, Consolidated Foods changed its name to Sara Lee Corporation, after one of its most respected brand names, and Kiwi changed its name to Kiwi Brands.

Ingredients

Natural and synthethic waxes, solvents (to soften waxes and allow them to be spread on leather), oil-soluble dyes (to stain leather), pigments (to add color)

Strange Facts

■ Nearly 80 percent of all corporate executives believe that well-cared-for shoes are very important to a person's success.
■ New Zealand is the only place kiwi birds are found in the wild.
■ Because the kiwi is the national emblem of New Zealand, pictures of the kiwi are found on money, stamps, and coins.
■ The kiwi has wings but cannot fly. Its beak is a third the length of its body, and its nostrils are at the tip of that beak.

A five-pound kiwi lays an egg that weighs just over a pound—a record in the bird kingdom.

Distribution

■ Kiwi is the best-selling shoe polish in the world.

■ Kiwi Brands also makes Kiwi Shine Wipes, Kiwi Clean Gleam, Kiwi Twist 'n Shine, Kiwi Scuff Zapper, Kiwi Wet Pruf, Kiwi Protect All, and Kiwi Sneaker Shampoo.

■ Kiwi Brands' parent company, Sara Lee, makes Bali intimate apparel, Champion activewear, Coach leather goods, Hanes hosiery and apparel, L'eggs panty hose, Playtex intimate apparel, Ball Park frankfurters, and Endust no-wax dusting spray.

For More Information

Kiwi Brands, Douglassville, PA 19518-1239. Or telephone 1-610-385-3041. On the Internet, visit www.kiwicare.com.

Krazy Glue

■ **Lessen the pain of paper cuts.** Apply Krazy Glue to paper cuts to relieve the pain. The Krazy Glue deprives the nerve endings of air, according to *The Doctor's Book of Home Remedies II.*

■ **Repair a broken fingernail.** Use a small drop of Krazy Glue to secure the nail in place, then coat with nail polish.

■ **Remove ticks from inside the ear of a horse, cow, dog, or cat.** Put a drop of Krazy Glue on a broom straw, apply it to the tick, and pull it right out.

■ **Reattach a broken heel or loose tassels.** Use a few drops of Krazy Glue and hold in place until secure.

■ **Fix leaks in inflatable inner tubes, air mattresses, or air pillows.** Apply Krazy Glue to seal the hole or leaky valve stems.

■ **Prevent bra pads from slipping.** Use Krazy Glue to attach Velcro to the inside cups of the bra and the outside of the pads.

Invented

1963

The Name

Krazy Glue is named for the glue's seemingly crazy strength, quick-setting properties, and longevity as an adhesive.

A Short History

In 1963, Toagosei Co., Ltd., a Japanese chemical company founded in 1942 in Tokyo, began producing the instant adhesive Aron Alpha. The product is distributed in the United States as Krazy Glue by Elmer's Products, Inc., a Borden Incorporated Company. Borden Inc., a dairy company founded in 1857 by Gail Borden Jr. in Burrville, Connecticut, had also become a glue manufacturer by 1929.

Ingredients

Modified ethyl cyanoacrylate

Strange Facts

■ In the motion picture *What About Bob?* (1991), Dr. Leo Marvin (Richard Dreyfuss) describes the symbiotic Bob Wiley (Bill Murray) as "human Krazy Glue."

■ If your fingers get stuck together with Krazy Glue, dissolve the bond with nail polish remover or acetone, or soften with warm soapy water.

■ The winners of the 1996 "How Krazy Glue Saved the Day" contest, Don McMullan and Sharon Bennett of Clearwater, British Columbia, used Krazy Glue to get themselves down Robber's Pass when their eighteen-wheel semi-trailer's engine cooling fan separated from its rotating shaft hundreds of miles from the nearest service station in the middle of the night. They put six drops of Krazy Glue on the two metal pieces, held the parts together securely for three minutes, and were back on the road for another eighty thousand miles.

■ Surgeons treat an arterial venous fistulas, or entangled cluster of arteries, by injecting liquid acrylic agents into the abnormal blood vessels to seal off the excessive flow of blood. The material used, n-butyl cyanoacrylate, is similar to the ingredients in Krazy Glue.

■ Physicians in Canada use an adhesive similar to Krazy Glue instead of stitches, lowering the possibility of bacterial infection and minimizing scarring.

■ During her highly publicized disappearance for four days in April 1996, Margot Kidder, who costarred with Christopher Reeve in the Superman movies, lived inside a cardboard box with a homeless person in downtown Los Angeles while suffering a manic-depressive episode. According to *People* magazine, "Kidder had lost some caps on her front teeth that sometimes fell out and which she cemented back in place with Krazy Glue. 'When you're having a manic episode,' she says, 'you don't always remember to pack the Krazy Glue.'"

■ Food stylists use Krazy Glue to keep food in place during photography sessions for advertisements, television commercials, and motion pictures.

Distribution

■ Elmer's Products, Inc., which distributes Krazy Glue in the United States, also makes a variety of other consumer adhesives, including Elmer's Glue-All and Elmer's School Glue, as well as wood fillers and caulk.

For More Information

Elmer's Products, Inc., 180 East Broad Street, Columbus, OH 43215.

McCormick/Schilling

Black Pepper

■ **Stop small leaks in a car radiator.** Add a teaspoon of McCormick/Schilling Black Pepper to your radiator. The pepper sinks to the bottom, finds its way into small holes, and expands, filling them.

■ **Repel moths.** Use McCormick/Schilling Black Pepper as an alternative to mothballs. Fill a cheesecloth bag or the foot of a nylon stocking with pepper and use it as a sachet.

■ **Stop colors from running.** Add a teaspoon of McCormick/Schilling Black Pepper to the first suds when you are washing cottons.

■ **Keep dogs, raccoons, cats, and other animals away from your garden.** Sprinkle McCormick/Schilling Black Pepper around your hedges and flower beds.

■ **Repel ants.** Sprinkle McCormick/Schilling Black Pepper in cracks and crevices.

■ **Enhance the flavor of ice cream.** *McCormick/Schilling's New Spice Cookbook* recommends softening one quart vanilla or chocolate ice cream just enough to stir (without allowing it to melt), spooning it into a large bowl, and adding one tablespoon crushed green peppercorns, one teaspoon coarse ground black pepper, and one-quarter teaspoon coconut extract. Then eat.

Invented

A natural product, black pepper was most likely incorporated into the McCormick spice line during the 1896 acquisition of F. G. Emmett Spice Company.

The Name

McCormick & Company is named for company founder Willoughby McCormick.

A Short History

In 1889, twenty-five-year-old Willoughby McCormick founded McCormick & Company—crafting fruit syrups, root beer, and nerve and bone liniment in his Baltimore home—and hired three salesmen to peddle his wares door-to-door. A year later, the company was making food coloring, cream of tartar, and blood purifier. In 1896, McCormick bought the F. G. Emmett Spice Company of Philadelphia, firmly committing itself to the spice industry. By the turn of the century, McCormick was regularly trading with the East and West Indies, South Africa, Europe, and Central and South America. The company achieved coast-to-coast distribution in 1947 with the acquisition of A. Schilling & Co., producers of spices and extracts.

Strange Facts

■ In 80 B.C., Alexandria, Egypt, became the greatest spice trading port of the eastern Mediterranean, with one of its entrances known as "Pepper Gate."

■ In A.D. 410, Alaric the Visigoth demanded one and a half tons of pepper as ransom from Rome. Two years later, he started receiving three hundred pounds of pepper annually from the city.

■ During the Middle Ages in Europe, pepper was counted out peppercorn by peppercorn.

■ In the eleventh century, many towns kept their accounts in pepper. Taxes and rents were assessed and paid in pepper. A sack of pepper was worth a man's life.

■ Between 1784 and 1873, the pepper trade furnished a huge portion of the import duties collected in Salem, Massachusetts, at one point financing 5 percent of the entire United States government's expenses.

■ At the turn of the century, unscrupulous spice dealers would cut shipments of peppercorns with mouse droppings.

■ The Russians sprinkle pepper on vodka.

Ingredients

Pure ground black pepper

Distribution

■ McCormick is the world's largest spice company.

■ The company's seasonings are sold under the McCormick brand name in the eastern U.S., the Schilling brand in the West, and under the Club House label in Canada.

■ McCormick/Schilling also makes cream of tartar, food coloring, spices, seasoning, and vanilla extract.

For More Information

McCormick & Company, Inc., 18 Loveton Circle, Sparks, MD 21152. Or telephone 1-410-771-7301.

Miracle Whip

Salad Dressing

■ **Condition your hair.** Apply one-half cup Miracle Whip to dry hair once a week as a conditioner. Leave on for thirty minutes, then rinse a few times before shampooing thoroughly.

■ **Remove a ring stuck on a finger.** Smear on some Miracle Whip and slide off the ring.

■ **Give yourself a facial and tighten pores.** Miracle Whip helps moisten dry skin when applied as a face mask. Wait twenty minutes, then wash it off with warm water followed by cold water.

■ **Remove white rings and spots from wood furniture.** Wipe on Miracle Whip, let stand for an hour, and polish the furniture.

■ **Remove tar.** Spread a teaspoon of Miracle Whip on tar, rub, and wipe off.

■ **Treat minor burns.** Rub Miracle Whip into the burn. Let it set, then wipe off.

■ **Soothe sunburn and windburn pain.** Use Miracle Whip as a skin cream.

■ **Remove dead skin.** Rub a dab of Miracle Whip into your skin and let it dry for a few minutes. While the skin is moist, massage with your fingertips. Dead skin will rub off your feet, knees, elbows, or face.

■ **Remove chewing gum from hair.** Rub a dollop of Miracle Whip into the chewing gum.

Invented
1933

The Name
The word *miracle* presumably refers to the whip's endless uses rather than to any supernatural properties.

A Short History
In the eighteenth century, French Duc de Richelieu discovered a Spanish condiment made of raw egg yolk and olive oil in the port town of Mahón on the island of Minorca, one of the Balearic Islands. He brought the recipe for "Sauce of

Mahón" back to France, where French chefs used it as a condiment for meats, renaming it *mayhonnaise*.

When mayonnaise arrived in the United States in the early 1800s, it was considered a haute French sauce, too difficult to prepare. The invention of the electric blender and the advent of bottled dressings catapulted mayonnaise into the mainstream as a sandwich spread. In 1912, Richard Hellmann, a German immigrant who owned a delicatessen in Manhattan, began selling his premixed mayonnaise in one-pound wooden "boats," graduating to glass jars the following year.

To compete with Hellmann's mayonnaise, J. L. Kraft and Bros. Co., a cheese wholesaling business started in Chicago by James Lewis Kraft in 1903, purchased several regional salad dressing companies during the 1920s and introduced Kraft brand mayonnaise in 1930.

During the Depression, when mayonnaise became a luxury item, Kraft introduced Miracle Whip—a spoonable dressing that combined the best features of both mayonnaise and boiled dressing—at the 1933 Chicago World's Fair. The Kraft exhibit attracted millions of visitors, and within seven months, Miracle Whip, advertised on the Kraft Music Hall radio program, became the best-selling salad dressing in America.

Ingredients

Soybean oil, water, vinegar, sugar, egg yolks, starch, food starch-modified, salt, mustard flour, spice, paprika, natural flavor

Strange Facts

■ In 1991, Kraft sold enough Miracle Whip to make 3.8 billion servings of potato salad.

■ Miracle Whip contains less fat and 30 percent fewer calories than mayonnaise.

■ The Miracle Whip Chocolate Cake, developed by consumers during World War II food rationing, has been the most requested recipe from the Kraft Kitchens.

■ Kraft celebrated the fiftieth anniversary of Miracle Whip in 1983 at the Waldorf-Astoria in New York City with a five-foot-high cake in the shape of a Miracle Whip salad dressing jar—complete with the famous red, white, and blue label.

Distribution

■ Miracle Whip has been the best-selling salad dressing in the United States since 1933.

■ Kraft introduced Miracle Whip Light reduced-calorie salad dressing in 1984 and Miracle Whip Free nonfat dressing in 1991.

For More Information

Kraft Foods, Inc., One Kraft Court, Glenview, IL 60025. Or telephone 1-800-543-3733.

Mint Waxed Floss

■ **Truss poultry for cooking.** Fill the cavity with stuffing, cross the two legs, and tie legs together with Oral-B Mint Waxed Floss. If necessary, sew the cavity closed.

■ **Repair the mesh screening on playpens.** Sew up the rip with Oral-B Mint Waxed Floss.

■ **Cut a birthday cake.** Oral-B Mint Waxed Floss cuts cake into neat slices.

■ **Lift cookies from a cookie sheet.** Slide a strand of Oral-B Mint Waxed Floss between fresh-baked cookies and the cookie sheet.

■ **Repair a tent or backpack.** When hiking or camping, Oral-B Mint Waxed Floss makes a durable, strong thread for tough repairs.

■ **Sew buttons on heavy coats.** Use Oral-B Mint Waxed Floss as a durable thread.

■ **Hang pictures, sun catchers, or wind chimes.** Oral-B Mint Waxed Floss is stronger and more durable than ordinary string.

■ **String beaded necklaces.** Oral-B Mint Waxed Floss is

thin enough for small beads, yet stronger than thread.

■ **Slice cheese.** Oral-B Mint Waxed Floss cuts neatly through cheese for clean slices.

Invented
1994

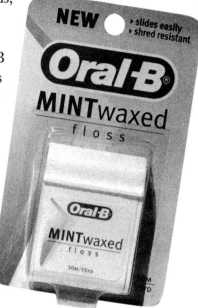

The Name
Dental floss is a simple combination of the words *dental* and *floss*, stemming from the Latin word *dentalis* and the Danish word *vlos*.

A Short History
The early Egyptians used thread as dental floss, but Johnson & Johnson received the first patent for a woven silk dental floss in 1876. In 1896, Johnson & Johnson made dental floss commercially available in waxed and unwaxed silk. In 1940, at the recommendation of Dr. Charles Bass, Johnson & Johnson switched from silk to nylon. In the 1940s, periodontist Robert Hutson invented Oral-B toothbrushes, the first multitufted, soft-nylon bristle toothbrushes. In 1984, Gillette branched into dental products with the purchase of Oral-B.

Ingredients

Nylon, plastic, wax, mint

Strange Facts

■ Merriam-Webster, Inc., added the verb *floss* to its dictionary in 1974.

■ According to Johnson & Johnson, roughly 55 percent of all flossers floss one or more times daily. Of those individuals, 14 percent floss before breakfast, 26 percent floss between breakfast and lunch, 19 percent floss between lunch and dinner, 32 percent floss after dinner, and 67 percent floss just before going to bed.

■ Approximately 80 percent of all dental floss consumers prefer waxed floss products.

■ Women tend to floss more than men, and people over fifty years of age tend to floss more than children and young adults.

Distribution

■ Consumers purchase more than 3.5 billion yards of dental floss every year.

■ Oral-B is the world's leading producer of dental care products.

■ In 1995, Oral-B sold over $441 million worth of products.

For More Information

Oral-B Laboratories, Redwood City, CA 94065. Or telephone 1-415-598-5000.

Toothbrush

■ **Clean the grout between bathroom tiles.** Use a clean, old Oral-B Toothbrush to scrub the grout clean.

■ **Make a spatter painting.** Place a piece of paper inside a small cardboard box and place leaves, stencils, or flowers on the paper. Cover the opening of the box with a sheet of metal screening secured in place with rubber bands. Dip the Oral-B Toothbrush in paint and scrub it over the screen, allowing the paint to spatter over the paper. Remove the screen and various objects, and let the painting dry.

■ **Stake up small plants.** Use the handles from old Oral-B Toothbrushes.

■ **Give a manicure or pedicure.** A clean, old Oral-B Toothbrush dipped in soapy water is both gentle and effective for cleaning fingernails and toenails.

■ **Neutralize car battery acid to facilitate cleaning.** Use an old toothbrush to scrub encrusted battery terminals clean with a paste made from three parts baking soda to one part water.

■ **Clean typewriter keys.** Scrub the keys with a clean, old Oral-B Toothbrush dipped in alcohol.

■ **Unblock small appliance vents.** Gently clear lint and dust from the vent with a clean, old Oral-B Toothbrush.

■ **Clean artificial flowers and plants.** Use a clean, old Oral-B Toothbrush and soapy water.

■ **Clean crevices.** Use a clean, old Oral-B Toothbrush with silver polish to remove tarnish from silver.

■ **Groom your eyebrows.** Use a clean, old Oral-B Toothbrush.

■ **Clean combs.** Dip a clean, old Oral-B Toothbrush in alcohol and scrub the teeth of the comb.

■ **Clean the blade of an electric can opener.** Unplug the can opener and use a clean, old Oral-B toothbrush dipped in alcohol to clean the blade.

■ **Clean a food grater.** Scrub the grater with a clean, old Oral-B toothbrush dipped in dishwashing liquid.

■ **Clean a motor.** Dip a clean, old Oral-B Toothbrush in kerosene or mineral spirits to remove gunk from crevices.

Invented
1940s

The Name

Oral-B is a combination of *oral* hygiene and the letter *B*, which stands for the word *better*.

A Short History

The nylon-bristle toothbrush is a descendant of the "chew stick," a twig with a frayed end of soft fibers that was rubbed against the teeth to clean them. Chew sticks have been found in Egyptian tombs dating to 3000 B.C. The first bristled toothbrush, made from bristles plucked from the backs of hog's necks and fastened to bamboo or bone handles, originated in China in 1498. Traders from the Orient introduced Europeans to the practice of brushing their teeth, and the few Europeans who adopted the practice opted for horsehair toothbrushes, though most preferred the Roman toothpick. After Du Pont chemists discovered nylon in the 1930s, the company marketed the first nylon-bristle toothbrush in 1938.

In the 1940s, periodontist Robert Hutson invented Oral-B Toothbrushes, the first multitufted, soft-nylon bristle toothbrushes. In 1984, Gillette acquired Oral-B, enabling Oral-B to make its toothbrushes available in virtually every country in the world.

Ingredients

Nylon, plastic

Strange Facts

■ In 1937, the year before Du Pont introduced the first nylon-bristle toothbrush, the United States imported 1.5 million pounds of hog bristles for toothbrushes.

■ According to the American Dental Association, 80 percent of all Americans fail to replace their toothbrush until after the bent bristles are no longer fit for cleaning teeth.

■ Oral-B Toothbrushes incorporate the features recommended by dental professionals: a long narrow neck designed for more effective brushing of back teeth; a thumb grip for better maneuverability; a rounded head for greater comfort; and polished, end-rounded bristles to help protect gums and tooth enamel.

■ Oral-B Indicator bristles fade as the brush wears out.

Distribution

■ Oral-B is the world's leading producer of dental care products.

■ Oral-B Toothbrushes are used by more dentists and hygienists worldwide than any other toothbrushes.

■ Oral-B Toothbrushes are available in straight and angled handles, and in a variety of head sizes and bristle textures.

■ In 1995, Oral-B sold over $441 million worth of products.

For More Information

Oral-B Laboratories, Redwood City, CA 94065. Or telephone 1-415-598-5000.

Pink Pearl

Eraser

■ **Clean piano keys.** Use a Pink Pearl Eraser to remove marks from the ivory keys.

■ **Fix a wobbly table.** Cut a Pink Pearl Eraser to fit the bottoms of the table legs and affix with nails or glue.

■ **Remove scuff marks from floors.** Simply use a Pink Pearl Eraser.

■ **Prevent framed pictures from tilting or scratching the wall.** Glue at least two Pink Pearl Erasers to the bottom edge of the back of the frame.

■ **Improvise a pincushion.** In a pinch, keep needles, pins, and safety pins stuck in a Pink Pearl Eraser.

■ **Erase fingerprints from woodwork.** Gently rub with a Pink Pearl Eraser.

■ **Prevent throw rugs from skidding.** Glue thin slices of a Pink Pearl Eraser to the bottom of the rug at the four corners.

■ **Clean cotton upholstery.** Rub lightly with a Pink Pearl Eraser.

■ **Store small drill bits.** Twist the bits point-first into a large Pink Pearl Eraser.

■ **Clean golf balls.** Pack a Pink Pearl Eraser in your golf bag.

■ **Clean gold.** The Pink Pearl Eraser gently scours gold-plated items such as pens and jewelry without damaging the material.

Invented
Circa 1890

The Name
Eberhard Faber commonly named its erasers after its pencils. At the time, Eberhard Faber already had a trademark on a pencil called the "Pearl" that was manufactured exclusively for F. W. Woolworth Company. Since the eraser was pink in color and the company already had rights to the "Pearl" name, Eberhard Faber decided to call it the "Pink Pearl" eraser.

A Short History
In 1848, Eberhard Faber, great-grandson of Casper Faber, who first produced and marketed lead pencils in Nuremberg, Bavaria, in 1761, came to America to establish an import

business that included Faber Pencils. In 1861, he started his own pencil factory in New York City. Upon Eberhard Faber's death in 1879, the business was passed down to his twenty-year-old son, John, who demonstrated his business savvy by promptly having his name legally changed to Eberhard Faber II. Eberhard II headed the company until his death in 1946. His nephew, Eberhard III, would have become the next president had he not died a year earlier trying to save the life of his son, Eberhard Faber IV, who was being pulled out to sea by an undertow (Eberhard IV was saved by his uncle, Duncan Taylor). Instead, Eberhard III's widow, Julia Faber, became the major owner of the firm, and ten years later, the company moved to Wilkes-Barre, Pennsylvania. In 1971, Eberhard Faber IV became president and chief executive officer of the company. In 1987, Faber-Castell Corporation purchased Eberhard Faber, and the following year the company's facilities were moved to Lewisburg, Tennessee. In 1994, Newell Co. bought Faber-Castell and merged with Sanford Corporation.

Ingredients

Synthetic rubber, factice (a soybean-based filler), and pumice

Strange Facts

■ Eberhard Faber founded the United States's first pencil factory in New York City in 1861 on the present site of the United Nations building. After being destroyed by a fire in 1872, the pencil plant was relocated to Brooklyn's Greenpoint section.

■ Pumice, a volcanic ash from Italy, helps the rubber erase

and gives it more erasing power. The unique formulation of rubber and factice gives the Pink Pearl its distinctive aroma and also makes it softer than any other eraser in the world.

■ Eberhard Faber was the first company to put erasers on pencils. The idea caught on in the United States immediately, but it has never caught on in Europe. Europeans claim they shun the practice because pencils with erasers encourage schoolchildren to be careless. Students (and just about everyone else in Europe) use separate erasers.

■ A poor or abrasive eraser actually loosens and removes the paper fibers. A well-formulated eraser like the Pink Pearl erases by cleaning the paper surface.

Distribution

■ In 1996, Eberhard Faber sold more than 4.7 million Pink Pearl Erasers. Laid end to end, that's enough erasers to reach from Washington, D.C., to Philadelphia.

■ Sanford, the company that owns Eberhard Faber, is the world's largest manufacturer of pencils.

For More Information

Sanford, 551 Spring Place Road, Lewisburg, TN 37091. Or telephone 1-800-323-0749.

Reddi-wip

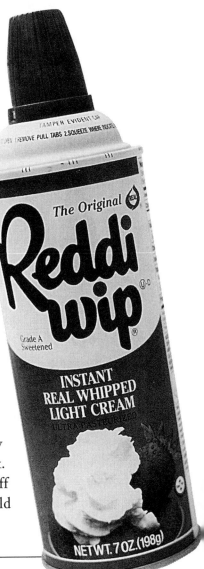

■ **Lighten coffee.** Use a table-spoon of Reddi-wip as a substitute for milk or cream in a cup of coffee.

■ **Shave.** Apply Reddi-wip to wet skin as a substitute for shaving cream.

■ **Condition your hair.** Apply one-half cup Reddi-wip to dry hair once a week as a conditioner. Leave on for thirty minutes, then rinse a few times before shampooing thoroughly.

■ **Make a sour cream substitute.** Mix three or four drops of lemon juice with one cup Reddi-wip and let sit for thirty minutes.

■ **Give yourself a moisturizing facial.** Reddi-wip helps moisten dry skin when applied as a face mask. Wait twenty minutes, then wash it off with warm water followed by cold water.

■ **Soothe a burn on the roof of your mouth from hot pizza.** Fill your mouth with Reddi-wip to coat the lesion. Press the Reddi-wip gently against the roof of your mouth with your tongue. Repeat if necessary.

■ **Remove makeup.** Wet face with lukewarm water, spread a handful of Reddi-wip on face, rinse clean with lukewarm water, and blot dry.

■ **Improve marital relations.** Give new meaning to the phrase "dessert topping."

Invented
1948

The Name
Reddi-wip calls your attention to the fact that the whipped cream is ready to use because it's already whipped.

A Short History
In 1941, 28-year-old Aaron "Bunny" Lapin, a Washington University drop-out selling shirts and socks in his father's clothing emporium in St. Louis, Missouri, went to Chicago to visit his brother-in-law, Mark Lipsky, who was in the milk business. In Lipsky's outer office sat a man trying to sell a product called "Sta-Whip," a substitute whipping cream made of light cream and vegetable fat, held together with a secret chemical stabilizer. Whipping cream, which contains a minimum of 30 percent butterfat, was not made during

World War II because war-time restrictions prohibited the manufacture of cream containing more than 19 percent butterfat. At Lapin's suggestion, his brother-in-law bought the rights to the Sta-Whip formula and handed over the business to Lapin.

Lapin returned to St. Louis and made a deal with Valley Farm Dairy. The dairy would make Sta-Whip, Lapin would sell it, and they'd split the profits.

Lapin convinced local bakeries to try making whipped cream cakes with Sta-Whip, and within two weeks, Lapin was making more money with his substitute whipping cream than he was in the clothing store. He then sold his first franchise to Louis Lang, a veteran dairy man in St. Louis, who made the product, sold it in bulk to bakers and in containers to housewives, and paid Lapin royalties.

To avert the slump in whipping cream sales during the summer months, Lapin had a "gun" designed which drug store soda fountain jerks could use to squirt Sta-Whip on ice cream sodas.

To prevent a container of Sta-Whip from spoiling before it could all be used, Lapin decided to develop a disposable pressure-propelled can to dispense Sta-Whip. Fortunately, the process had already been developed. In 1931, Charles Goetz, a senior chemistry major at the University of Illinois, worked part-time in the Dairy Bacteriology Department improving milk sterilization techniques. Convinced that storing milk under high gas pressure might inhibit bacterial growth, Goetz began experimenting—only to discover that milk released from a pressurized vessel foamed. Realizing that cream would become whipped cream, Goetz began seeking a gas that would not saturate the cream with its own bad flavor. At the suggestion of a local dentist, Goetz succeeded in infusing cream with tasteless, odorless, nonflam-mable nitrous oxide, giving birth to aerosol whipped cream and aerosol shaving cream.

In 1947, Lapin persuaded the Knapp-Monarch Co., an appliance manufacturer in St. Louis, to can his whipped cream—renamed Reddi-wip—and to develop a special nozzle to trap the gas that whips the cream inside the can, forcing out only whipped cream. The next year, Lapin set up Reddi-wip as a corporation, and by 1951, the company was doing $7 million in business.

Ingredients

An ultrapasteurized blend of cream, skim milk, whey, sugar, corn syrup, mono- and diglycerides, natural and artificial flavors, carrageenan, whipping gas—nitrous oxide

Strange Facts

■ In the 1950s, Reddi-wip, Inc. tried to develop aerosol ketchup, aerosol shampoo, aerosol mayonnaise, aerosol mus-tard, and aerosol iodine.

■ Reddi-wip, Inc. sponsored the Arthur Godfrey radio show.

■ Company founder Aaron Lapin was nicknamed "Bunny" by his classmates at the University of Washington after they learned that his last name means rabbit in French.

■ In 1988, at an erotic art exposition in Moscow, a woman was covered in whipped cream and men in the audience were invited to lick it off, according to *Time* magazine.

Distribution

■ Reddi-wip is available in Instant Real Whipped Light Cream, Deluxe Instant Real Whipped Heavy Cream, Fat Free Whipped Topping, and Non-Dairy Whipped Topping.

For More Information

Visit Reddi-wip on the internet at www.beatricecheese.com. Or write Beatrice Cheese, Inc., Waukesha, WI 53186. Or telephone 1-414-782-2750.

Saran Wrap

■ **Create a miniature greenhouse to help seeds germinate.** Lay a sheet of Saran Wrap over four Popsicle sticks inserted into a seed tray. The Saran Wrap creates a tiny greenhouse, providing enough humidity to keep the growing medium moist for germination. If too much moisture collects on the inside of the plastic, remove it for a few hours.

■ **Protect a book cover.** Use a sheet of Saran Wrap to protect a dust jacket.

■ **Temporarily repair a window.** Tape Saran Wrap over a small hole to keep out wind, rain, or snow.

■ **Hold a screw in position.** Push the screw through a small piece of Saran Wrap, fit the screwdriver into the groove in the head, gather up the edges of the Saran Wrap and hold back over the blade of the screwdriver, and screw.

■ **Prevent a layer of skin from forming inside a paint can.** Place a sheet of Saran Wrap over the open paint can before tapping the lid closed with a hammer.

Invented

1953

The Name

Saran, the trademark name for vinylidene chloride polymer, was made up by Dow chemists, who added the word *Wrap* to clarify the new plastic's purpose.

A Short History

Swiss chemist and businessman Jacques Brandenberger invented cellophane and spent the next ten years developing the machinery to mass-produce his invention. In 1908, he patented the manufacturing process, and in 1911, he began selling cellophane, named from cellulose (the wood pulp derivative used to make the film) and the Greek word *diaphanes* ("transparent"). Coating cellophane with polyvinylidene chloride gives the film the lowest gas and moisture transmission.

Meanwhile, in Midland, Michigan, Herbert Dow had developed a process in 1897 to use electricity to extract bromides and chlorides from underground brine deposits. He founded Dow Chemical, and the company's first product was chlorine bleach. In the 1940s, Dow research yielded synthetic plastics, leading to the introduction of Saran Wrap, the company's first major consumer product, in 1953. Plastics and silicone products boosted sales, catapulting Dow to the forefront of U.S. companies with sales topping $1 billion in 1964. Today polyvinylchloride and polypropylene films have replaced cellophane in almost every use where heat is not present.

Ingredient
Plastic film

Strange Facts
■ When Carl Reiner asked Mel Brooks as the 2,000-Year-Old Man to name the greatest invention in the history of the world, Brooks replied, "Saran Wrap."

■ The unique composition of Saran Wrap provides the highest temperature tolerance and resistance to hot fats and oils, making it the best product for use in a microwave oven. It is strong enough to go directly from the freezer to the microwave without melting or tearing. (Always turn back one corner of the plastic wrap to let excess steam escape during cooking. And never use any plastic wrap to microwave foods with a high sugar content. These foods can be extremely hot and may cause plastic wrap to melt.)

■ Rumor contends that a piece of Saran Wrap can be used as an impromptu condom. It does not work. Plastic film does not withstand the friction of sexual intercourse, nor does it provide an adequate barrier against sperm.

Distribution
■ Dow operates 68 manufacturing plants in the United States and 115 plants in thirty-one foreign countries.

■ Dow, the nation's number-two chemical company (after Du Pont), also makes Ziploc Storage Bags, Handi-Wrap, Spray 'n Wash, and Dow Bathroom Cleaner.

For More Information

DowBrands L.P., P.O. Box 68511, Indianapolis, IN 46268-0511. Or telephone 1-800-428-4795.

Packaging Tape

■ **Cork a wine or champagne bottle.** Wipe the lip of the bottle dry and seal tightly with a small piece of Scotch Packaging Tape.

■ **Remove splinters.** Place Scotch Packaging Tape over the splinter and gently peel off.

■ **Remove fuzz, lint, and pet hair from clothing and furniture.** Wrap a strip of Scotch Packaging Tape around your hand, adhesive side out, and pat.

■ **Hold wires in place while soldering.** Use Scotch Packaging Tape.

■ **Clean a metal file.** Put a piece of Scotch Packaging Tape over the length of the file, press firmly, then peel off. The shavings will stick to the tape.

■ **Provide first aid in an emergency.** Bandage wounds with torn sheets and Scotch Packaging Tape, or make emergency splints with two-by-fours and Scotch Packaging Tape.

■ **Kill ants.** Use a strip of Scotch Packaging Tape to pick up an advancing line of ants.

■ **Repair clothes in an emergency.** Scotch Packaging

Tape will hold fabric together until you can find a needle and thread.

■ Tag the pull cord that opens the drapes. Wrap a half-inch piece of Scotch Packaging Tape at eye level around the right cord.

■ Remove dust balls from under a bed or couch. Wrap Scotch Packaging Tape, adhesive side out, to the end of a broomstick, and slide it under the furniture.

■ Detain   crooks. Wrap a captured thief or burglar securely to a chair with Scotch Packaging Tape, call 911, and wait for the police.

■ Remove a broken windowpane. Wearing gloves, crisscross Scotch Packaging Tape on both sides of the broken glass, tap the inside edges with a hammer until the pane breaks free, then peel off the tape to remove any shards.

■ Secure the lid on a barbecue grill for transportation purposes. Simply use Scotch Packaging Tape.

■ Repair torn book covers. Adhere the cover back to the binding with Scotch Packaging Tape.

- **Organize cables and extension cords.** Tape the cords together with Scotch Packaging Tape.

- **Prevent picnic tablecloths from blowing away.** Tape the corners to the table with Scotch Packaging Tape.

- **Reinforce game and puzzle boxes.** Fortify the corners of boxes with Scotch Packaging Tape.

- **Attach loose speakers to a boom box.** Use Scotch Packaging Tape.

- **Label suitcases.** Write your name and address on two index cards and use Scotch Packaging Tape to tape one card inside the suitcase and another on the outside.

- **Hang any item on a pegboard.** Fold a piece of Scotch Packaging Tape over the edge of any small object, punch a hole in the tape, and hang on a peg.

- **Repair a broken taillight.** Use Scotch Packaging Tape to hold the translucent red plastic in place.

- **Fix a frayed shoelace tip.** Wrap the frayed end with a small strip of Scotch Packaging Tape.

- **Repair a disposable diaper.** If the adhesive tab doesn't stick, tape the diaper together with Scotch Packaging Tape.

Invented
1940

The Name

The name Scotch tape actually resulted from an ethnic slur foisted upon manufacturers of the tape—although the product does not have any connection with Scotland or the Scottish.

In 1925, the automobile industry, eager to satisfy Americans' craving for two-tone cars, had difficulty making a clean, sharp edge where one color met another. Richard Drew, a 25-year-old laboratory employee primarily involved with abrasives used to make sandpaper at the Minnesota Mining and Manufacturing Company (better known as 3M), developed a two-inch-wide strip of paper tape coated with a rubber-based adhesive. To cut costs, he had the masking tape coated with only a strip of glue one-quarter-inch wide along each edge, instead of coating the entire two-inch width.

Unfortunately, the tape failed to hold properly, and the painters purportedly told the 3M salesman, "Take this tape back to those Scotch bosses of yours and tell them to put adhesive all over the tape, not just on the edges." The 3M Company complied, but when the salesman returned to the automobile paint shop, a painter derogatorily asked him if he was still selling that "Scotch" tape, launching a trade name based on an ethnic slur denoting stinginess. The name, like the improved tape, stuck.

A Short History

In 1929, the Flaxlinum Company asked 3M to develop a water- and odor-proof tape to seal the wrapping on insulation slabs in railroad refrigeration cars. Drew coated Du Pont's new moisture-proof cellophane with a rubber-based adhesive, which, while not strong enough for insulation slabs, was marketed to the trade as Scotch Tape—"the only natural, transparent, quick seal for 'Cellophane.'" Since then, the 3M Company has developed more than nine hundred kinds of pressure-sensitive tapes from Drew's invention, including Scotch Packaging Tape.

Ingredients

Polypropylene, adhesive

Strange Fact

■ 3M produced a gold reflective Scotch tape that was used in a lunar landing vehicle as insulation against the temperature extremes of space.

Distribution

■ Scotch brand tapes also include Scotch Transparent Tape, Scotch Mailing Tape, and Scotch Strapping Tape.

For More Information

3M Consumer Stationery Division, P.O. Box 33594, St. Paul, MN 55133. Or telephone 1-800-364-3577.

Scotchgard

■ **Make ski pants.** Spray a pair of old jeans with Scotchgard. Be sure to wear long underwear for warmth.

■ **Protect white gloves.** Spray with Scotchgard before you wear them.

■ **Preserve sewing patterns.** Spray a new pattern with Scotchgard to prevent rips, tears, and wrinkles.

■ **Waterproof an umbrella.** Spray the fabric on an umbrella with Scotchgard so water runs off with a quick shake, allowing the umbrella to dry faster.

■ **Waterproof tents, backpacks, and sleeping bags.** Stay dry during a camping trip by spraying your gear with Scotchgard.

■ **Protect mattresses from bed wetters.** Spray mattresses with Scotchgard to resist moisture.

■**Keep schoolbooks and supplies dry inside a student's backpack.** Spray the outside of a student's backpack with Scotchgard.

■**Protect neckties from spills.** Spray ties with Scotchgard so spills roll right off.

Invented
1956

The Name
Scotchgard is a combination of the words *Scotch*, meaning "Scotsman," and a misspelling of *guard*, meaning "to protect."

A Short History
In 1902, 3M was started by five businessmen in Two Harbors, Minnesota, to sell corundum to manufacturers of grinding wheels. When that failed, the company moved to Duluth and converted an old flour mill to a sandpaper factory, eventually moving to St. Paul in 1910. The company introduced Scotch brand masking tape in 1925, followed by Scotch brand cellophane tape in 1930.

In 1944, 3M bought the rights to a process for producing fluorochemical compounds. The company's researchers could not find any practical uses for the process or its reactive, fluorine-containing by-products—until a laboratory assistant accidentally spilled a sample of the substance on one of her tennis shoes. The assistant could not wash the stuff off with water or hydrocarbon solvents, and the stained spot on her tennis shoe also resisted soiling. Two 3M chemists, Patsy Sherman and Sam Smith, realized that this substance might be used to make textiles resist water and oil stains, and went to work to enhance the compound's ability to repel liquids, giving birth to Scotchgard.

Dr. Richard Smith, the son of Sam Smith, led a team of scientists working to eliminate the ozone-depleting chemical methyl chloroform in the product his father developed. In 1994, 3M introduced the new water-based Scotchgard.

Ingredients
Naphthol spirits, carbon dioxide, heptane, fluoroalkyl polymer, petroleum distillate, trichloroethane

Strange Fact
■ 3M voluntarily phased out most uses of chlorofluorocarbons (CFCs) and other Class I ozone-depleting chemicals in its operations worldwide by the end of 1992, four years before the United States government mandate for 1996.

Distribution
■ In 1977, there were nearly thirty formula variations for Scotchgard for protecting materials including furniture fabrics, wall coverings, luggage, and carpets.

For More Information
3M Home & Commercial Care Products, P.O. Box 33068, St. Paul, MN 55133. Or telephone 1-800-364-3577.

Drink Mix

■ **Clean toilet bowls.** Put Tang in the toilet bowl and let it sit for one hour. Brush and flush. The citric acid in Tang removes stains from porcelain.

■ **Clean your dishwasher.** Put Tang in the detergent cup and run the machine through its normal cycle. The citric acid in Tang removes grunge and soap scum from the inside of a dishwasher.

■ **Shampoo your hair.** The citric acid in Tang cuts through sebum oil in hair.

■ **Spice up your baking.** Add Tang to your cake and cookie mixes for an "orange zest."

■ **Make a space-age screwdriver.** Mix Tang with vodka.

■ **Cook with Tang.** The Kraft Consumer Center offers a free packet of recipes, including Orangey Pancakes (made with one-half cup of Tang), Whipped Orange Butter (requiring two tablespoons of Tang), Oriental Barbecue Sauce (using one-third cup of Tang), and Herbed Orangey Dressing (made with three tablespoons Tang and one envelope of Good Seasons Classic Herb Salad Dressing Mix).

Invented
1959

The Name
Tang is short for *tangy* and also suggests the flavor of tangerine.

A Short History
Following the introduction of instant coffee and powdered milk, General Foods decided to create a breakfast beverage from a powder that required no refrigeration, mixed with water into single servings, and provided the taste of real orange juice and all the same vitamins. Scientists at the Post Division of General Foods struggled to infuse the powder with stable, water-soluble forms of vitamin A, develop an orange coloring, and prevent the powder from caking in the jar.

Ingredients
Sugar, fructose, citric acid (provides tartness), calcium phosphate (prevents caking), potassium citrate (controls acidity), ascorbic acid (vitamin C), orange juice solids, natural flavor,

titanium dioxide (for color), xanthan and cellulose gums (provide body), yellow 5, yellow 6, niacinamide, artificial flavor, vitamin A palmitate, vitamin B_6, riboflavin (vitamin B_2), BHA (preserves freshness), folic acid

Strange Facts

■ In 1965, Tang accompanied the astronauts on the Gemini spaceflights, and Tang has been on all United States space-flights through to the *Apollo 11* moon landing in 1969, helping Tang garner a reputation as a nutritionally balanced futuristic food.

■ On *Saturday Night Live*, Mrs. Loopner (Jane Curtin) and her daughter, Lisa Loopner (Gilda Radner), drank Tang by the pitcher. Beldar Conehead (Dan Aykroyd) consumed mass quantities of the orange powder dry and straight from the jar.

Distribution

■ Tang holds an 85 percent share in the instant breakfast drink category.

For More Information

Kraft Foods, Inc., Box 6Q-TJA, White Plains, NY 10625. Or telephone 1-800-431-1002.

Converted Brand Rice

■ **Remedy intestinal disorders.** Eating plain Uncle Ben's Converted Brand Rice will help cure diarrhea, according to *Prevention* magazine.

■ **Prevent moisture from clumping up salt.** Add a few grains of uncooked Uncle Ben's Converted Brand Rice to the salt shaker to absorb excess moisture.

■ **Make a maraca for children.** Put a handful of uncooked Uncle Ben's Converted Brand Rice inside a clean, empty milk carton, and seal the carton shut with Scotch Packaging Tape. Let the child decorate the milk carton with glitter, plastic jewels, and shapes cut from construction paper.

■ **Clean stains from a thermos bottle.** Pour in a tablespoon of uncooked Uncle Ben's Converted Brand Rice and a cup of warm water. Shake vigorously, then rinse.

Invented
1943

The Name
In the 1940s, rice farmers in Houston, Texas, rated their rice against the rice grown by a local farmer named Uncle Ben. Frank Brown, a maître d' in a Houston restaurant, posed for the portrait of Uncle Ben.

A Short History
During the processing necessary to produce white rice, the bran layer—containing a large part of the nutritive value of rice—is removed. In England, scientists discovered a special steeping and steaming process to force the bran nutrients, under pressure, into the rice grain *before* the bran is removed, locking the nutrients inside the grain.

In the early 1940s, George Harwell, a successful Texas food broker, received permission to introduce the process developed in England to the United States—but only if he could build a plant immediately. Because the new process improved the nutritional, cooking, and storage qualities of a food that had remained unchanged for more than five thousand years, Harwell convinced the United States government that this unique product merited war priorities. In 1943, Harwell and his partners shipped the first carload of Converted Brand Rice to an army quartermaster depot.

Until the end of World War II, Converted Brand Rice was produced for use solely by military personnel. Then in 1946, Harwell's company, Converted Rice, Inc., brought this special rice to American consumers for the very first time, using the familiar portrait of Uncle Ben as its trademark. Consumer response was so great that in just six years Uncle Ben's Converted Brand Rice became the number-one packaged long-grain rice sold in the United States.

Ingredients

Long-grain parboiled rice enriched with iron (ferric orthophosphate) and thiamine (thiamine mononitrate)

Strange Facts

■ The original Uncle Ben was a black rice farmer known to rice millers in and around Houston for consistently delivering the highest quality rice for milling. Uncle Ben harvested his rice with such care that he purportedly received several honors for full-kernel yields and quality. Legend holds that other rice growers proudly claimed their rice was "as good as Uncle Ben's." Unfortunately, further details of Uncle Ben's life (including his last name) were lost to history.

■ In the 1980s, the company dropped Uncle Ben from the rice boxes for two years. Sales plummeted, and the company quickly reinstated Uncle Ben's portrait on the boxes.

■ The world's leading producer of rice is China. The world's leading exporter of rice is Thailand, followed by the United States. The world's leading importer of rice is Iran.

■ Adding one tablespoon of butter, margarine, or oil to the water before adding the rice will prevent the rice from becoming sticky.

■ To reheat cooked rice, put it in a coffee filter placed in a vegetable steamer and heat over boiling water.

- Rice is thrown at weddings as a symbol of fertility.
- Rice is grown on more than 10 percent of the earth's arable surface.
- Rice is the mainstay for nearly 40 percent of the world's population.
- Uncle Ben's Converted Brand Rice retains up to 85 percent of the natural B-complex vitamins, giving it more natural food value than ordinary white rice.
- In 1995, Houston Rockets basketball star Hakeem Olajuwon agreed to be a spokesperson for Uncle Ben's.

Distribution

- Uncle Ben's is the world's leading parboiled rice brand.
- Uncle Ben's rices include Uncle Ben's Converted Brand Original Rice, Uncle Ben's Brand Instant Rice, Uncle Ben's Brand Boil-in-Bag Rice, Uncle Ben's Brown Rice, Uncle Ben's Long Grain and Wild Rice, Uncle Ben's Country Inn Recipes Rice Dishes, and Uncle Ben's Country Inn Recipes Pasta and Sauce Dishes.

For More Information

Uncle Ben's, Inc., P.O. Box 1752, Houston, TX 77251. Or telephone 1-713-674-9484.

Tennis Balls

■ **Store valuables.** Make a two-inch slit along one seam of a Wilson Tennis Ball, then place valuables inside. If you hide the doctored tennis ball among your other sports equipment, remember not to use it.

■ **Fluff your down jacket in the dryer and reduce static cling.** Throw in a handful of Wilson Tennis Balls to fluff the down while the jacket is tumbling in the dryer.

■ **Childproof the sharp corners of furniture.** Cut old Wilson Tennis Balls into halves or quarters and use Scotch Packaging Tape to affix the sections over sharp corners of coffee tables, end tables, cabinets, dining room tables, and other pieces of furniture that might be dangerous to a small child.

■ **Make parking cars in your garage easier.** Hang a Wilson Tennis Ball on a string from the garage ceiling so it will hit the windshield at the spot where you should stop your car.

■ **Prevent a chrome trailer hitch from getting scratched.** Slit a Wilson Tennis Ball and put it over the trailer hitch as a protective cover.

■ **Make a walker glide more easily.** Cut a hole in two Wilson Tennis Balls and fit them on the back feet of the walker.

■ **Give yourself a foot massage.** Roll your foot over a Wilson Tennis Ball.

■ **Remove cobwebs from unreachable places.** Wrap a Wilson Tennis Ball inside a dust cloth secured with a few rubber bands, then toss at the distant cobweb.

■ **Play "basket tennis."** Remove the bottom of an empty coffee can, and nail the can above the garage door. Use a Wilson Tennis Ball to play basketball.

■ **Strengthen your grip.** Squeeze a Wilson Tennis Ball in each hand.

■ **Prevent snoring.** Sew a Wilson Tennis Ball inside a pocket on the back of your pajama top to prevent you from sleeping on your back.

■ **Prevent a deck chair from slipping through the cracks of a dock.** Slit four Wilson Tennis Balls and fit them on the feet of the deck chair.

■ **Make a back massager.** Put several Wilson Tennis Balls inside a sock and tie the sock at the end. This type of massager is frequently used by a labor coach to massage the back of a woman in labor.

■ **Keep your car door open without wasting the battery.** Wedge a Wilson Tennis Ball into the doorjamb to depress the interior light switch.

Invented
1914

The Name
When the Ashland Manufacturing Company was forced into receivership in 1914, a group of bankers decided to rename the company Wilson and Company to capitalize on President Woodrow Wilson's popularity at the time.

A Short History
In 1913, the Chicago-based meat-packing firm of Schwartzchild and Sulzberger created the Ashland Manufacturing Company as a subsidiary to sell violin strings, surgical sutures, and strings for tennis rackets—all by-products of animal gut. The company soon branched out into making tennis rackets, camping equipment, fishing tackle, bicycles, automobile tires, and phonographs.

In 1914, a New York banking firm took over the company and selected Thomas E. Wilson, a vice president of the meat-packing firm, to manage the company. The bankers chose Wilson because they had already decided to rename the company Wilson and Company to capitalize on President

Woodrow Wilson's popularity. Thomas E. Wilson began expanding the company by purchasing other sporting goods companies that manufactured baseball masks, tennis rackets, baseballs, baseball gloves, and uniforms.

The company also went through a number of name changes until 1931, when it became known as Wilson Sporting Goods Co. In the 1940s, Wilson created an advisory staff of sports figures who field-tested equipment and offered suggestions on improving it. In 1970, PepsiCo purchased the company, and in 1989, Wilson was acquired by Amer Group Ltd., an international conglomerate based in Helsinki, Finland, and involved in marketing motor vehicles, paper, communications, and tobacco.

Ingredients
DuraWeave felt, high-grade wool, copolymer fibers, rubber, adhesive, ink

Strange Facts
■ In 1930, a can of three Wilson Tennis Balls sold for $1.50 in the Sears & Roebuck catalog. In 1990, that same can of balls sold for less than $2.

■ Once a Wilson Tennis Ball is removed from its pressurized can, the rebound of the balls decreases over time due to pressure loss. The rebound loss, however, is only between .032 and .038 inches per day.

■ Wilson is the only ball used at all United States Tennis Association national championships.

■ Since 1979, Wilson has been the official ball of the U.S. Open.

- A number between one and eight is imprinted on each Wilson Tennis Ball to help players keep track of their tennis balls while playing.
- Wilson Tennis Balls are packaged in specially designed, 100 percent recyclable, pressurized containers capable of keeping the balls fresh for years when unopened.
- Duraweave is an exclusive Wilson felt developed with high-grade wool uniquely interwound with copolymer fibers to form a tight, uniform weave. The result is a long-lasting tennis ball with enhanced play and consistency.
- According to United States Tennis Association specifications, tennis balls must weigh between 2 and 2.06 ounces, measure between 2.575 and 2.7 inches in diameter, and when dropped from a height of 100 inches onto a solid, concrete base, rebound to a height of between 53 and 58 inches.

Distribution

- Wilson Tennis Balls are sold throughout the world, including France, Germany, England, Japan, Singapore, Hong Kong, and Latin American countries.
- Wilson also makes tennis rackets, tennis shoes, footballs, basketballs, baseball gloves, golf clubs, and golf balls.

For More Information

Wilson Sporting Goods Co., 8700 West Bryn Mawr Avenue, Chicago, IL 60631. Or telephone 1-800-WIN-6060.

Wonder Bread

■ **Clean wallpaper.** Use two-day-old crustless slices of Wonder Bread to rub down the wallpaper.

■ **Remove corns.** Make a poultice of one crumbled piece of Wonder Bread soaked in one-quarter cup Heinz Vinegar. Let poultice sit for one-half hour, then apply to the corn and tape in place overnight. If corn does not peel off by morning, reapply the poultice for several consecutive nights.

■ **Deodorize a stale lunch box.** Soak a piece of Wonder Bread in Heinz Vinegar and leave it inside the closed lunch box overnight.

■ **Erase pencil marks from paper.** Ball up a small piece of Wonder Bread (without the crust) and use it as you would an eraser.

Invented
1921

The Name
Elmer Cline, the Taggart Baking Company vice president appointed to merchandise a new one-and-a-half-pound loaf bread, was awed by the sight of the sky filled with hundreds

of colorful hot-air balloons at the International Balloon Race at the Indianapolis Speedway. The wonder of that sight prompted Cline to name the new bread Wonder Bread, and colorful balloons have been featured on the Wonder Bread wrappers ever since.

A Short History

In 1921, Taggart Baking Company of Indianapolis, Indiana, decided to go along with a postwar trend to bring out a one-and-a-half-pound loaf of bread. To promote the new bread's debut, company trucks delivered helium-filled balloons to children in Indianapolis neighborhoods. Messages attached to the balloons urged mothers to try new Wonder Bread. Continental Baking Company bought Taggart in 1925, and Wonder Bread soon became a national brand. In 1930, Wonder Bread was introduced in sliced loaves to a first suspicious, then enthusiastic, public. In 1996, Interstate Bakeries Corporation (IBC) acquired Continental Baking Company, making IBC the largest wholesale baker of fresh delivered bread and cake in the United States.

Ingredients

Enriched wheat flour (barley malt, niacin, iron [ferrous sulfate], thiamin mononitrate, riboflavin), water, high-fructose corn syrup, yeast, contains 2 percent or less of: salt, vegetable oil (contains one or more of: canola oil, corn oil, cottonseed oil, soybean oil), soy flour, calcium sulfate, sodium stearoyl lactylate, monoglycerides, starch, yeast nutrients (ammonium sulfate), leavenings (monocalcium phosphate), vinegar, wheat gluten

Strange Facts

■ Continental Baking Company was not the only producer of Wonder Bread. The Seven Baker Brothers Co. of Pittsburgh also produced a bread named Wonder, and there was some dispute as to which company had used the brand name first. When the Pittsburgh company went out of business around 1930, Continental bought the trademark rights.

■ In 1941, Continental Baking Company joined in the government-supported bread-enrichment program, adding vitamins and minerals to Wonder Bread. Known as the "quiet miracle," bread enrichment nearly eliminated beriberi and pellagra and brought essential nutrients to people who previously could not afford nutritious foods.

■ Wonder Bread does not contain any cholesterol or saturated fat.

■ Wonder Bread has been endorsed on television by Howdy Doody and Buffalo Bob, and was praised in song by the Happy Wonder Bakers quartet.

■ In the 1970s, Continental Baking Company became the first national wholesale baking company to print freshness dates and nutritional information on bread product wrappers. The move came at a time when the whole-grain bread revolution threatened to erode white bread's market share.

■ In 1986, Continental Baking Company introduced Wonder Light, with only forty calories per slice, compared with approximately seventy-five calories per slice of regular bread.

■ In 1993, the New York State record black bullhead catfish was caught at Wantagh Mill Pond with a piece of Wonder Bread.

■ In 1996, artist Michael Gonzalez's show at the Huntington Beach Art Center featured paintings incorporating Wonder Bread wrappers.

■ In his book, *The Total Package*, design critic Thomas Hine compares the Wonder Bread wrapper with the monstrance, the ornate container that holds the bread used in Roman Catholic liturgy. According to Hine, the monstrance calls attention to the invisible presence of Christ within the bread; the Wonder Bread wrapper calls attention to the invisible nutritional additives advertised to build strong bodies twelve ways.

Distribution

■ Wonder Bread is the best-selling bread in the United States.

■ Thousands of loaves of fresh Wonder Bread are distributed to store shelves on more than seven thousand delivery routes from Continental's forty bakeries across the country.

■ Interstate attributes Wonder Bread's popularity to the company's continuing commitment to freshness, consistent product quality, and colorful merchandising and advertising campaigns.

For More Information

Interstate Brands Corporation, P.O. Box 419627, 12 East Armour Boulevard, Kansas City, MO 64111. Or telephone 1-816-502-4000.

And Much, Much More

Phillips'®
Milk of Magnesia

Minimize oily skin. Apply Phillips' Milk of Magnesia as a thin mask over your face, let dry, then rinse off with warm water. **For More Information:** The Charles H. Phillips Co., Bayer Corporation, Consumer Care Division, Gulfport, MS 39501. Or telephone 1-800-331-4536.

Preparation H®

Prevent shaved horse hair from growing back white. Apply Preparation H to the shaved skin of the horse every day until the hair grows back properly. **For More Information:** Whitehall-Robbins Healthcare, 1 Campus Drive, Parsippany, NJ 07054. Or telephone 1-201-660-5500.

Slinky®

Improvise a radio or television antenna. During the Vietnam War, communications soldiers would toss a Slinky over a high tree branch as a makeshift radio antenna.

For More Information: James Industries, Inc., Beaver Road Extension, Hollidaysburg, PA 16648. Or telephone 1-814-695-5681.

If you know more offbeat uses for brand-name products, send your tips and suggestions to:
Joey Green
Wash Your Hair with Whipped Cream
c/o Hyperion
114 Fifth Avenue
New York, NY 10011

Acknowledgments

My editor Laurie Abkemeier once again fought coura-geously for my right to share hundreds of offbeat uses for brand-name products with the American public. I deeply admire her contagious enthusiasm, keen sense of humor, and unbridled love for American ingenuity.

I am also grateful for the extraordinary talents of Samantha Miller, Claudyne Bedell, Victor Weaver, Bob Miller, Liz Kessler, Adrian James, Jeremy Solomon, Kim from L.A., Bob Baskinsherry, and a battalion of copy-editors and proof-readers.

In corporate America, I am indebted to Daniel Stone at Alberto Culver (makers of VO5), Carol Alberti and Christine Ervin at Bayer Corporation (makers of Alka-Seltzer and Phillips' Milk of Magnesia), David Worrell at Church & Dwight, Inc. (makers of Arm & Hammer Baking Soda), Janet Silverberg at the Quaker Oats Company (makers of Aunt Jemima Original Syrup), Arthur Moore, Marsha Erickson, Joyce Reid, and Edie Burge at Avery Dennison (makers of Avery Laser Labels), Richard Cahill at Pfizer, Inc. (makers of Barbasol), Karen Preble at Whitehall-Robins and Ronald Alice and Steven H. Flynn at American Home Products (makers of ChapStick), Georgianna Mandelos at Marina Maher (public relations firm for Cover Girl), Mary Jon Dunham at Procter & Gamble (makers of Cascade and Crisco), Robert Alexander at James River Corporation (mak-ers of Dixie Cups), Susan Meyer at Sara Lee Corporation (makers of Endust and Kiwi shoe polish), Thomas Knuesel at Diamond Brands (makers of Forster Toothpicks), Bruce Stein, Benton Spayd, and Arthur Coddington at Mattel (makers of Frisbee), Gary Wamer at First Brands Properties (makers of GLAD Flexible Straws), William Perlberg at Hartz Mountain Corporation, Boyd Tracy at Kimberly-Clark (makers of Huggies baby wipes), Sharon Ptak Miles at Kraft Foods, Inc., (makers of Jell-O, Miracle Whip, and Tang), Tom Boyden at GCI Group (public relations firm for Krazy-Glue), Richard LeBlanc at Krazy Glue, Diane Hamel at McCormick & Company, Inc., Kerry Gleeson at Oral-B Laboratories, Robert Parker and Donna King at Sanford Corporation (makers of Pink Pearl Eraser), Leslie Tripp at Beatrice Cheese (makers of Reddi-wip), Lauren Cislak at DowBrands (makers of Saran Wrap), Judy Schuster at 3M (makers of Scotch Packaging Tape and Scotchgard), Olin Hoover, Marlene Machut, and Bertille Glass at M&M Mars (makers of Uncle Ben's Converted Brand Rice), Ray Berens at Wilson Sporting Goods, Co., Mark Dirkes at Interstate Brands Corporation (makers of Wonder Bread), Karen Brown at Whitehall-Robins (makers of Preparation H), and Betty James at James Industries (makers of Slinky).

Upstanding Americans who shared their ingenuity include Robert and Barbara Green, Lora and Barry Schwartzberg, Amy and Robin Robinson, Adam Turteltaub, Allan and Andrea Brum, Anne Allen McGrath, John Fiorre Pucci, and the dancing feet of Chris Spear.

Above all, all my love to Debbie, Ashley, and Julia.

The Fine Print

Sources

■ *All-New Hints from Heloise* by Heloise (New York: Perigee, 1989)

■ *Another Use For* by Vicki Lansky (Deephaven, MN: Book Peddlers, 1991)

■ *Ask Anne & Nan* by Anne Adams and Nancy Walker (Brattleboro, VT: Whetstone, 1989)

■ *Can You Trust a Tomato in January?* by Vince Staten (New York: Simon & Schuster, 1993)

■ *A Dash of Mustard* by Katy Holder and Jane Newdick (London: Chartwell Books, 1995)

■ *Dictionary of Trade Name Origins* by Adrian Room (London: Routledge & Kegan Paul, 1982)

■ *The Doctors Book of Home Remedies* by the Editors of *Prevention* Magazine (Emmaus, PA: Rodale Press, 1990)

■ *The Doctors Book of Home Remedies II* by Sid Kirchheimer and the Editors of *Prevention* Magazine (Emmaus, PA: Rodale Press, 1993)

■ *Encyclopedia of Pop Culture* by Jane and Michael Stern (New York: HarperCollins, 1992)

■ *Famous American Trademarks* by Arnold B. Barach (Washington, D.C.: Public Affairs Press, 1971)

■ *Hints from Heloise* by Heloise (New York: Arbor House, 1980)

■ *Hoover's Company Profile Database* (Austin, TX: The Reference Press, 1996)

■ *Household Hints & Formulas* by Erik Bruun (New York: Black Dog and Leventhal, 1994)

■ *Household Hints for Upstairs, Downstairs, and All Around the House* by Carol Reese (New York: Henry Holt and Company, 1982)

■ *Household Hints and Handy Tips* by *Reader's Digest* (Pleasantville, NY: Reader's Digest Association, 1988)

■ *How the Cadillac Got Its Fins* by Jack Mingo (New York: HarperCollins, 1994)

■ *Kitchen Medicines* by Ben Charles Harris (Barre, MA: Barre, 1968)

■ *Make It Yourself* by Dolores Riccio and Joan Bingham (Radnor, PA: Chilton, 1978)

■ *Mary Ellen's Best of Helpful Hints* by Mary Ellen Pinkham (New York: Warner/B. Lansky, 1979)

■ *Mary Ellen's Greatest Hints* by Mary Ellen Pinkham (New York: Fawcett Crest, 1990)

■ *Our Story So Far* (St. Paul, MN: 3M, 1977)

■ *Panati's Extraordinary Origins of Everyday Things* by Charles Panati (New York: HarperCollins, 1987)

■ *Practical Problem Solver* by *Reader's Digest* (Pleasantville, NY: Reader's Digest, 1991)

■ *Rodale's Book of Hints, Tips & Everyday Wisdom* by Carol Hupping, Cheryl Winters Tetreau, and Roger B. Yepsen Jr. (Emmaus, PA: Rodale Press, 1985)

■ *Symbols of America* by Hal Morgan (New York: Viking, 1986)

■ *Why Did They Name It . . . ?* by Hannah Campbell (New York: Fleet, 1964)

■ *The Woman's Day Help Book* by Geraldine Rhoads and Edna Paradis (New York: Viking, 1988)

Trademark Information

"Alberto VO5" is a registered trademark of Alberto-Culver USA, Inc.

"Alka-Seltzer" is a registered trademark of Miles, Inc.

"Arm & Hammer" is a registered trademark of Church & Dwight Co., Inc.

"Aunt Jemima" is a registered trademark of the Quaker Oats Company.

"Avery" is a registered trademark of Avery Dennison Corporation.

"Barbasol" and "Beard Buster" are registered trademarks of Pfizer Inc.

"Cascade" is a registered trademark of Procter & Gamble. Photograph used by permission.

"ChapStick" is a registered trademark of American Home Products Corporation.

"Cover Girl" and "NailSlicks" are registered trademarks of Noxell Corp.

"Crisco" is a registered trademark of Procter & Gamble. Photograph used by permission.

"Dixie" is a registered trademark of James River Corporation.

"Endust" is a registered trademark of Sara Lee Corporation.

"Forster" is a registered trademark of Forster Manufacturing Company, Inc.

"Frisbee" is a brand name and a registered trademark of Mattel, Inc., used with permission. Mattel, Inc. makes no endorsement of the uses of Frisbee discs other than as sports toys.

"GLAD" is a registered trademark of First Brands Corporation.

"Hartz" is a registered trademark of Hartz Mountain Corporation.

"Huggies," "Kleenex," and "Cleans Like a Washcloth" are registered trademarks of Kimberly-Clark Corporation.

"Jell-O" is a registered trademark of Kraft Foods, Inc. Photograph used with permission.

"Kiwi" is a registered trademark of Sara Lee Corporation.

"Krazy" is a registered trademark of Borden, Inc.

"McCormick" and "Schilling" are registered trademarks of McCormick & Company, Inc.

"Miracle Whip" is a registered trademark of Kraft Foods, Inc. Photo-

Index

removing crayon, Arm & Hammer Baking Soda, 24

Water spots
Endust, 66

Wax, removing
Alberto V05 Conditioning Hair-dressing, 6

Weather vane
Dixie Cups, 60

Weddings, rice alternative
Hartz Parakeet Seed, 80

Wind chimes
Oral-B Mint Waxed Floss, 106

Windburn, soothing
Arm & Hammer Baking Soda, 22
Miracle Whip, 102

Window
lubricating, Alberto V05 Conditioning Hairdressing, 4; Chap-Stick, 48
repairing, Saran Wrap, 122; Scotch

Packaging Tape, 127

Wine Jell-O
Jell-O, 87

Wood
cleaning, Alberto V05 Conditioning Hairdressing, 5; Pink Pearl Eraser, 113
staining, Kiwi Shoe Polish, 91

Wooden cutting board
Crisco, 56

Wooden salad bowls
Crisco, 56

Wrapping paper
Alberto V05 Hair Spray, 11

Wrestling
Jell-O, 87

Zipper, lubricating
Alberto V05 Conditioning Hairdressing, 3
ChapStick, 47

About the Author

Joey Green, author of *Polish Your Furniture with Panty Hose* and *Paint Your House with Powdered Milk*, got Jay Leno to shave with Jif peanut butter on the *Tonight Show*, had Katie Couric

drop her diamond engagement ring into a glass of Efferdent on the *Today* Show, and has been seen polishing furniture with SPAM on *CNN Headline News* and cleaning a toilet with Coca-Cola in the *New York Times*. A former contributing editor to *National Lampoon* and a former advertising copywriter at J. Walter Thompson, Green is the author of ten books, including *Selling Out: If Famous Authors Wrote Advertising, Hi Bob! (A Self-Help Guide to the Bob Newhart Show)*, and *The Partridge Family Album*. A native of Miami, Florida, and a graduate of Cornell University, he wrote television commercials for Burger King and Walt Disney World, and won a Clio Award for a print ad he created for Eastman Kodak. He backpacked around the world for two years on his honeymoon, and lives in Los Angeles with his wife, Debbie, and their two daughters, Ashley and Julia.

Get the Book That Started the Craze!

Informative, practical, and delightfully quirky, *Polish Your Furniture with Panty Hose*, the first volume of little-known uses for well-known products, tells you how to:

- Clean car battery corrosion with Coca-Cola®
- Soothe sunburn pain with Dannon® Yogurt
- Remove splinters with Elmer's® Glue-All
- Repulse deer with Ivory® soap
- Shave with Jif® peanut butter
- Fertilize a lawn with Listerine®
- Polish your furniture with SPAM®
- Lure trout with Vaseline® petroleum jelly

Dubbed a "modern day Heloise" by the *New York Times*, Joey Green will have you dancing in the supermarket aisles and roaring with laughter as you discover the histories behind the products, how they got their names, and, of course, the unbelievable ways they can be used.

In Bookstores Everywhere from Hyperion

As Seen on The Tonight Show

Polish Your Furniture With Panty Hose

And Hundreds of Offbeat Uses for Brand-Name Products

As Never Advertised on Television

Joey Green